Praise for *The SkiNy o*

This book boldly speaks about a topic that ... inclusion. Two fundamental issues that Pam McElvane has so eloquently brought light, hope, and clarity to in this unprecedented book. Her unique perspective and profound sharing outline why diversity and inclusion need to be honored, celebrated, and valued. This book will make a difference on a global scale.

—JB Owens, Founder and CEO of Ignite, Lotus Liners, and JBO Global Inc.

The SkiNy on Diversity Recruiting–Pam McElvane' s first installment of the SkiNy series–is a must-read vital resource for recruiting and sourcing in the diversity, equity, and inclusion world. From crafting strategy, to building a recruiting engine, to creating a sourcing plan, and implementing each component to achieve diversity goals, the book is more than just best practices–it's invaluable insight from one of the DEI movement's thought-leaders. All organizations should provide copies of this book to their HR and Recruiting Professionals.

—Edward Kopko, Author & CEO, Bold Business

Pam McElvane is a trusted resource for Corporate America seeking to recruit and retain the best and diverse talent. HACE is proud to support this book in ensuring that the workplace is well-equipped to recruit not only Latino talent, but talent from all diverse backgrounds. And this helps us get closer towards building inclusive and equitable workplaces for all.

—Patricia Mota, MPA, President & CEO, Hispanic Alliance for Career Enhancement (HACE)

This book is sure to become the new bible for results-driven diversity. For our company it has changed the way we communicate, recruit and design. Ms. McElvane and the data she presents demonstrates the financial windfall of diverse teams and her narrative explains what drives this. A must read.

—Dr. Mary Donohue, Author & CEO, The Digital Wellness Center

The SkiNy on Diversity Recruiting captures best practice action steps you can implement on targeted recruiting. This includes veterans, persons with disabilities and more. This book is not only informational, it serves as a toolkit with resources every manager and recruiter should own. As a DEI expert and thought leader, Pam McElvane simply displays the reality on what needs to happen to change the recruiting landscape.

—Nadine O. Vogel, CEO and Founder, Springboard Global Enterprises

The SkiNy on...

DIVERSITY RECRUITING

The Best Practice Guide to Current Trends on Recruiting Strategies

PAMELA A. McELVANE

The SkiNy on Diversity Recruiting: The Best Practice Guide to Current Trends on Recruiting Strategies

Cover jacket and book design by Sharee Dorsey, creativegrindstone.

Designed in the United States of America
ISBN 978-0-578-98149-9
First edition: October 2021

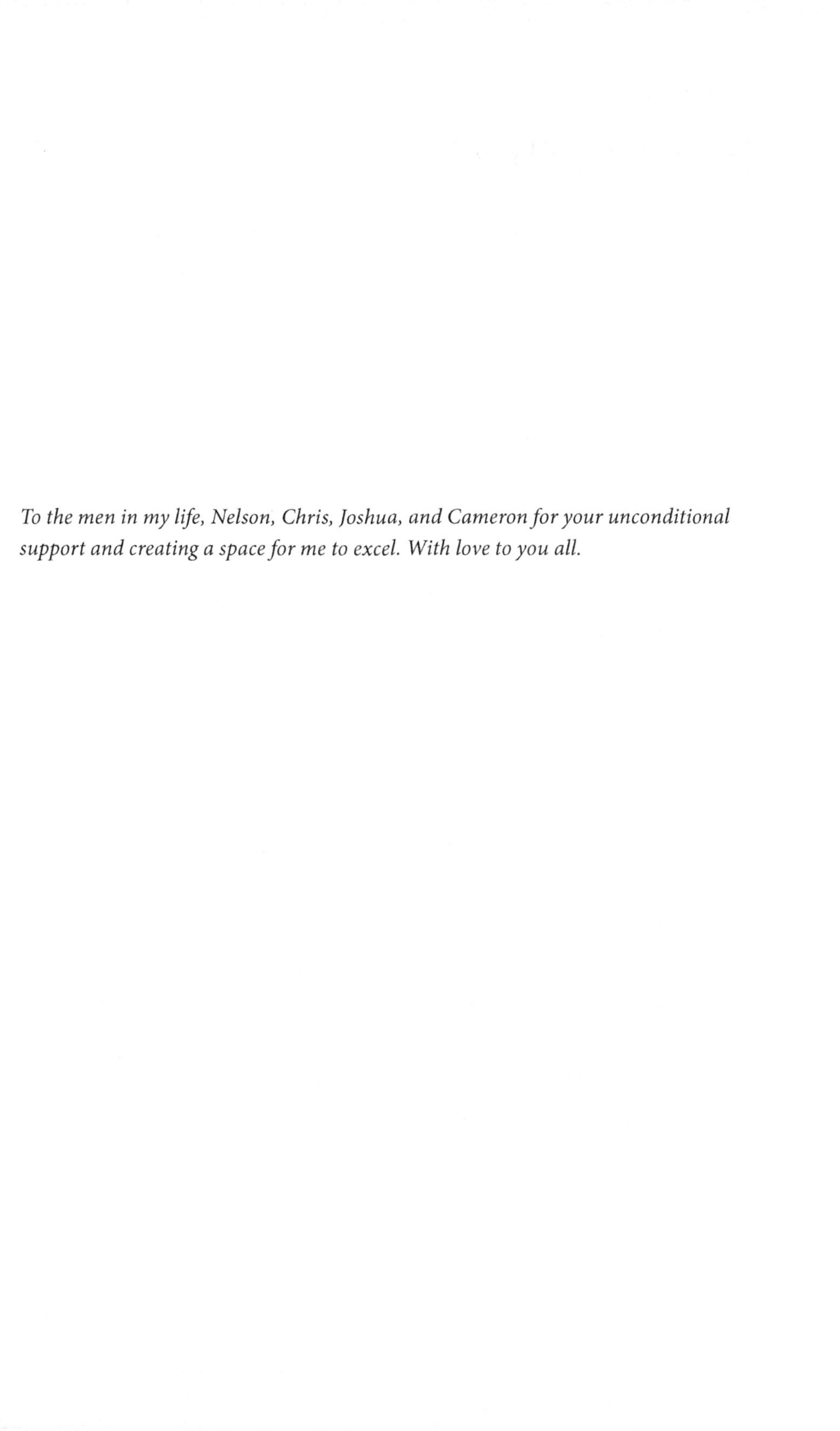

To the men in my life, Nelson, Chris, Joshua, and Cameron for your unconditional support and creating a space for me to excel. With love to you all.

CONTENTS AT A GLANCE

Table of Contents

Acknowledgments

The cliché "it takes a village," is the absolute truth when so many people for so long encouraged and supported me to put my insights and expert opinions in print, to be shared with everyone seeking a resource at their fingertips. While I want to specifically acknowledge everyone who has touched my life in one way or another, I must highlight those in my family who supported me unconditionally for years.

Nelson, my spouse, my friend, and life partner has believed in me and this work I am passionate about from the beginning. He has stood by my side with encouragement, vision, and insight. Nelson completes me. My three sons have been a primary source of motivation and contribution: Chris, Joshua, and Cameron. I have been blessed to have children who are smart, wise, innovative, and loving.

My very best friend, Karen Tolliver, has stood by me for more than 25 years, supporting all my ups and downs but keeping me spiritually connected. My Aunt Glenda and her family have been a steadfast source of family support, my brothers Anthony and Kenneth a great source of motivation; and finally, I am so grateful for the wisdom my Great Aunt Lula Langston, 93 years old, bestows upon me every day.

My team and partners are a combination of the most unselfish and committed people I have been blessed to know. Shout out to Patricia Forray, Sheila Howard, Dan Holly, TaVashané Brown, Chas Martin, Late Rhonda Grayson, Erika Young, Portia K. Smith, Jerry Thomas, Sheila Morgan, Cesar Rolan, Jorge Ortega, and Victor Powell.

While so many of my corporate and organization supporters have provided me such incredible insights and direction, I must acknowledge those that stayed the course in helping me realize my vision:

Alison Banks Moore, Horizon BCBS, Shield, NJ
Andres Gonzalez, Froedtert Health
Angela Foster Woods, NBMBAA
Angela Morris, Bank of America
Angela Roseboro, Riot Games
Angela Talton, Diversity & Operations Executive
Anise Wiley Little, Diversity & Executive
Anita Gonzalez-Scott, CTR Factor
Anthony Oliver, Entrepreneur
Belinda Grant Anderson, AT&T
Bishop Simon Gordon, Triedstone
Bridgett Hurd, BCBS, MI
Cynthia Bowman, Bank of America
David Bubas, UPMC
Deb Elam, Retired GE
Derrick Collins, Chicago State University
Donald Fan, Walmart
Dr. Andrea Hendricks, Cerner
Dr. Andrew Lee, Seattle Children's Hospital
Dr. Elizabeth Ortiz, DePaul University
Dr. Gloria Gipson, Northeastern University
Dr. James E. Taylor, UPMC
Dr. Kinneil Coltman, Atrium Health
Dr. Manika Turnbull, HCSC
Dr. Mary Chapman, WellStar Healthcare
Dr. Mary Donohue, Author & CEO
Dr. Patricia Arredondo, Arredondo Advisory
Dr. Ronald Copeland, Kaiser Permanente
Dr. Sue Fogel, DePaul University
Dr. Suri Surinder, CTR Factor
Ed Kopko, Bold Business
Erby Foster, Retired Clorox
Eugene Kelly, Colgate-Palmolive
Fernando Little, Atrium Health
Fred Hobby, Healthcare Executive
Erikajoy Daniels, Advocate Healthcare
George Halvorson, Retired CEO
Geri Thomas, Retired Bank of America
Grant Clarke, Face Book
Jahmal Miller, Dignity Health
Jetaun Mallet, Healthcare Management
Joshua Gustein, MBDA
Kathy Bowman Williams, Diversity
Keith Wyche, Best Selling Author
Kirsten Marriner, The Clorox Company
Larissa Williams, Diversity Executive
Magda Yizarry, Verizon Communications
Manuel Cuevas, Motorola Solutions
Marsha Jones, PNC Financial Services Group
Michael Escobar, Retired Allstate
Michael Millegan, Retired Verizon
Michael Wheeler, Diversity Executive
Miriam Lewis, Principal Financial Group
Monica Knox, Human Resource Executive
Nadine Vogel, Springfield Consulting
Neddy Perez, McCormick & Co
Peggy Harris, Atrium Health
Portia K. Smith, Recruiting Executive
Reginald Miller, McDonalds Corporation
Sharon Allen, Healthcare Executive
Sheila Morgan, Supplier Diversity Executive
Sherrin Ingram, Ingram, Author
Steve Humerickhouse, Workplace Forum
Tanya S. Blackmon, Novant Health
Tim Russell, Diversity Executive
Tom McCleary, Endow Inc.
Toni Carter, Diversity Executive

Foreword

Diversity Creates Strength—And Benchmarking Can Strengthen Diversity

There is a great strength to diversity. Diverse organizations are more creative, more innovative, and more synergistic at key functional levels. Diversity is an obvious asset to organizations.

We live in an increasingly diverse world, and diversity inside our organizations helps us at multiple levels. It helps us recruit more effectively and meet the needs of our customers with higher levels of performance.

As head of a health care system with roughly 200,000 employees and nearly ten million patients, I found that diversity in our staff helped us achieve goals that we would not have achieved as a less diverse organization.

Slightly more than 59 percent of our employees were from various minority groups. There was no majority group at Kaiser Permanente. How did we do with that level of diversity? We did well.

That highly diverse organization was rated number one in each of our markets by Consumer Reports and number one by JD Powers.

Medicare rated over 500 health plans in the country for more than 50 measures of quality and service. Medicare rated the plans with one to five stars for performance. Only 11 health plans in America were given all five stars. Eight of those five-star plans were Kaiser Permanente plans. All eight Kaiser Permanente plans were given the top rating by Medicare.

That meant that the most diverse health care organization in the country in its work force and its staff was rated the best in the country at quality of care and service to its members.

That high level of performance did not happen despite its diversity. It happened because of its diversity.

When an organization is clearly inclusive and celebrates its diversity—and when an organization is obviously a meritocracy because it promotes people from every group in the organization—then people in that setting perform at very high levels and feel satisfied being very good at doing what they do.

Creating a sense of internal community and internal alignment was key to that success. People love having a mission. People love being on teams. People love being with other good people who share a commitment to doing the right thing.

People love being diverse when the diversity is both celebrated and appreciated.

Benchmarking was a critical part of that process. Part of Kaiser Permanente's success in each of those areas came from benchmarking the quality of care and levels of service to members and patients.

Kaiser Permanente also benchmarked its diversity. Diversity benchmarking is very useful to do. *Diversity MBA* magazine has created some of the most useful and meaningful benchmarking tools for diversity—and those tools were part of the success story for Kaiser Permanente.

One of the ways we inspired and focused people in those areas was by competing in the annual diversity score card from *Diversity MBA* magazine. We competed so hard and so intentionally in that process that we were rated number one in the country for three straight years.

The Diversity MBA Media loved and supported what we did but wanted to be able to put another winner on their cover after three straight years, so they moved us to a brand-new *Diversity MBA* Hall of Fame that allowed other organizations to become the annual winner each year.

Even after going into the Hall of Fame, we continued to use key elements of the *Diversity MBA* benchmarking tools. We continued because this commitment to benchmarking gives us a wonderful tool for communicating our priorities to our employees.

Not only does benchmarking help structure both priorities and performance in key areas, it also helps us communicate and guide activities and performance in those areas.

Benchmarking makes figuring out key next steps easier for the people who lead organizations—and it allows organizations to build on the accumulated wisdom, insight, and development processes that contributed to the design of the actual benchmarks.

This book is a very good book to write right now and Pam McElvane, guru and top expert and advocate for benchmarking, is the perfect author. She has been a CEO for 20 years and is passionate about both inclusion and diversity, focusing on how women and people of color advance and are included in corporate America. She is a top national expert on those topics and a key designer and manager of benchmarking processes that have helped multiple organizations succeed in doing the necessary work to become more inclusive and diverse.

Her key insights provide other organizations with a road map to success. This book contains those insights and that guidance.

Pam is wise, insightful, articulate, deeply committed, and an excellent communicator who is doing us all a service by writing and sharing this book. Every company has the potential to become better in extremely important areas of performance as the result of what Pam shares in this book. I encourage everyone doing this work to read this book and use it as a resource that will be a change agent for getting this work done well.

Diversity works. Diversity—done well—is transformational; it changes many lives in very good ways. Enjoy the book, and celebrate the successes you will have as a result of Pam's coaching and wisdom.

by George Halvorson, Author, Retired Chairman & CEO Kaiser Permanente

Introduction

About the SkiNy Series

For more than a decade, Diversity MBA has been collecting original data to understand trends around talent management and diversity, equity, and inclusion strategy. The journey has been amazing. Every year, my team and I gain more insights and better understand current practices that companies are developing, experiencing, and pioneering.

Just to be clear, I came up with the SkiNy series as a way to establish a platform for seven books accompanied by a series of workbooks. Together, these works comprise the SkiNy series. The play on words is intended to be "The SkiNy on..." For example, The SkiNy on Recruiting... The SkiNy on Representation... and so on and so forth. It positions my research to be shared in topic format while providing the audience a connection with the header: now you have the SkiNy on the topic at hand. The spelling of "skinny" is intended to be different without any significant meaning behind the creativity of "SkiNy."

The question I have been trying to answer with some depth for many years is, "Why are Diversity, Equity, and Inclusion necessary?" I believe every person can answer this question differently. My answer is twofold: first, companies desire that their workforce mirror their customers and consumers; second, companies want to create a culture of belonging that celebrates the uniqueness of people's experiences and distinctions in the workplace. Culture is the single most impactful component. Regardless of how successful you are today, without intentional diversity, you will not achieve absolute cultural depth.

Why now am I writing a book about the intersection of talent management and diversity, equity, and inclusion? Basically, I just feel the time is right with my combination of experience and expertise I want to share with the global marketplace practical applications on achieving desired outcomes as they seek for more information on how to recruit, develop and retain talent.

The DMBA Inclusive Leadership Index (ILI) gathers research on seven key categories, then drills those categories down to fundamental levels. The data outcomes of the ILI are robust, practical, and realistic for application. Knowing how impactful the ILI results can be on an organization's culture when implemented, I decided to share this information through a series of books, the first of which you now hold in your hands. Each title in the series focuses on a specific topic of information and can be used as a quick, understandable, and easily accessible resource.

Also, in the past five years the surge of the popularity of Big Data has influenced the desire of leaders to review data in a very practical way as it relates to diversity and inclusion. The opportunity to break down the data and share it in a format that helps individuals interpret the data to use in creating actionable and measurable results. I hope you enjoy the first book in the series, *The SkiNy on Recruitment: The best practice guide to current trends on recruiting strategies*, and that you come to use it and others in the series as your professional resource.

About the Author

Not only has Pam McElvane built an organization that gathers data on an annual basis, she also is the expert who analyzes the data, meets with executives to gather insights on their experiences, and speaks to hundreds of audiences at all levels (including students, professionals, executives, and entrepreneurs). Pam has been communicating and sharing her original data through multiple media platforms so that thousands can have access to the real-time data that provides the most prolific insights and trends on what you can do—right now, today, *this moment*—to make changes that will impact the way you think and the way you work.

Pam McElvane has become one of the most respected thought leaders in the diversity, equity, and inclusion space. She has developed her craft for the past two decades by gathering and studying trends on how companies and organizations develop, design, and execute diversity and inclusion in their talent management strategies.

Pam's organization, Diversity MBA Media, has created a mobile app that allows easy and quick access to their information. They also publish monthly management and leadership publications that are another source of original content. Pam also is the author of a monthly blog, quarterly white papers, columns, and guest writer for many publications. She hosts her own radio show, *The Inclusive Voice* (820 AM WLT radio). She is constantly invited to speak at conferences, radio shows, lecture at universities and colleges, provide coaching to emerging leaders and act as trusted advisor to senior leaders. She is known as one of the most networked and highly resourced leaders today.

About the Research

Pam McElvane, CEO of Diversity MBA Media, has completed more than 14 years of benchmarking that has evolved into the ILI. The index is a survey designed to capture specific data from midsize to large companies and organizations as it relates to talent management, diversity, equity, and inclusion strategies, practices, methods, processes, metrics, and impact.

The survey application is managed by a third party that provides privacy protection for all companies that participate. Diversity MBA's website (www.diversitymbamagazine.com/benchmarking) hosts the registration form where companies can register to take the survey. After the registration form is completed, the DMBA research coordinator shares the actual survey to the registrant. The survey application process is open from January 15th to May 31st on an annual basis.

Companies participate in the survey application for two reasons. First, companies want to know how their diversity strategies and execution compare to top companies in the industry and in the marketplace. Second, they are interested in enhancing their reputation by hopefully achieving ranking status in the *Best Places to Work for Women and Diverse Managers* designation.

The ILI participation rates have increased year over year by 30 percent, consistently attracting 40 percent of new companies. The average size of the multinational participants is 35,000 employees, while the regional participants remain constant with an average size of 5,000 employees. That said, any company with at least 1000 employees is qualified to participate. More than 600 companies register to participate in the index, though only 300 companies qualify for index analysis to compete for the ranking. (All companies qualify for inclusion in the diver sity and industry benchmarking index.)

The methodology for the inclusive leadership index requires companies to complete 70 percent or more of the survey for it to qualify as primary research. Ninety percent or more of the survey must be completed to qualify for ranking in Best Places to Work for Women and Diverse Managers. This ranking is based on the scoring of six categories: *recruitment*, *representation*, *board diversity*, *workplace inclusion & retention*, *succession planning*, and *accountability*.

Through my data mining process, I can provide very detailed insights in each category, thus allowing me to provide a comprehensive perspective on each category. With more than 35,000 insights, there are insights for everyone at every level. The intent is to offer you ways to increase your personal awareness and understanding of Recruiting and Talent Acquisition best practices.

How This Book Is Organized

This book should be used as a frequent resource that will be readily accessible to anyone wanting to better understand how to recruit diverse talent. I selected the size of the book for quick and easy access. My intent is to ensure you can follow the sections of the book and effortlessly identify information needed to make decisions.

The exercises in the book are designed to get you thinking about what you need, to help you understand what you are doing, and to give you the ability to change what exists by adjusting your existing plan while building a best practice model for your company. The same template for developing a best practice has been implemented throughout the book so that it will become second nature to you when creating your own models.

This book is divided into four easily identifiable sections. Each section has three to four chapters that are all aligned with each section's subject. Each chapter focuses on one specific aspect of the subject matter with detail models and examples to help you build your diversity recruiting plan for your company. You can also go to the appendix to get resources aligned with each section of the book.

It is important for you to not only read and understand the changes in the marketplace and in your industry but for you to know how to create impact yourself.

My desire is for you to create a positive impact in your own workplace through selecting parts of the information held within these pages and implementing what is necessary into your environment as an actionable takeaway.

creating a flexible & agile diversity recruiting strategy

Part I

Chapter One

developing a flexible strategy: building the plan

"Sound strategy starts with having the right goal."
—Michael Porter, PhD

Is your diversity recruiting strategy aligned with your talent acquisition strategy? Of course, it is, why do you ask? I just want to make sure the goals you think are important and realistic are on track with the work the talent folks are doing.

Many experts, like Dr. Peter Drucker and Dr. Michael Porter, know that strategy begins with a goal that requires tactics to complete the plan. A good strategy should be simple and easily understood. Most importantly, a good strategy should be able to clearly complement the larger objective.

Strategy requires frequent and constant review; and from time to time needs to be adjusted to reflect what is really going on in the workplace. At the most fundamental level, a good strategy is one that allows you the ability to adjust without causing major disruption to the overall objective. This is the essence of flexibility.

As a general rule, organizations have an overall business strategy that focuses on gaining more customers and creating competitive advantages while ensuring the needs of their people are met. Strategies, like any other business component, must be cascaded down through multiple levels. This means that each business unit develops goals that are aligned to the overall business for that period.

The question I need to answer is, why do strategies to increase diversity also increase business success?

I believe there are three fundamental reasons CEOs want to increase diversity. First, to fulfill a promise to their consumers that their workforce will mirror their customer base with many elements of diversity. Second, companies recognize the importance of creating a culture of psychological safety and trust, which means bringing differences forward and truly respecting the authenticity of employee contributions. And third, CEOs value diversity as they understand that differences in experiences, cultures, and ideas contribute to innovation and lead to the creation of new products for new markets. For example, as a direct result of their diverse hiring practices, PepsiCo created the Guacamole tortilla and Jamaican chips, which created brand-new revenue streams into very specific markets.

At the very least, diversity as a business imperative supports innovation, creativity, productivity, and loyalty among all stakeholders. In today's environment, the moral compass is shifting when it comes to doing the right thing around diversity and inclusion.

To stay ahead of the curve, you must review your initiatives to ensure they are aligned with your strategic objectives, and be willing to pivot when the marketplace requires it.

Over the past five years, I have seen trends in the data collected for the index. There is an increase in the number of companies and/or organizations whose diversity and recruiting strategy has become aligned with their business strategy. You might ask, shouldn't this have always been the case? In an ideal world, yes; but the reality is that people tend to develop goals and plans in a vacuum. In today's information society, to gain a competitive advantage, you can no longer do things in a corner by yourself. It only takes two to form a team, but imagine having an entire village contributing to new ideas!

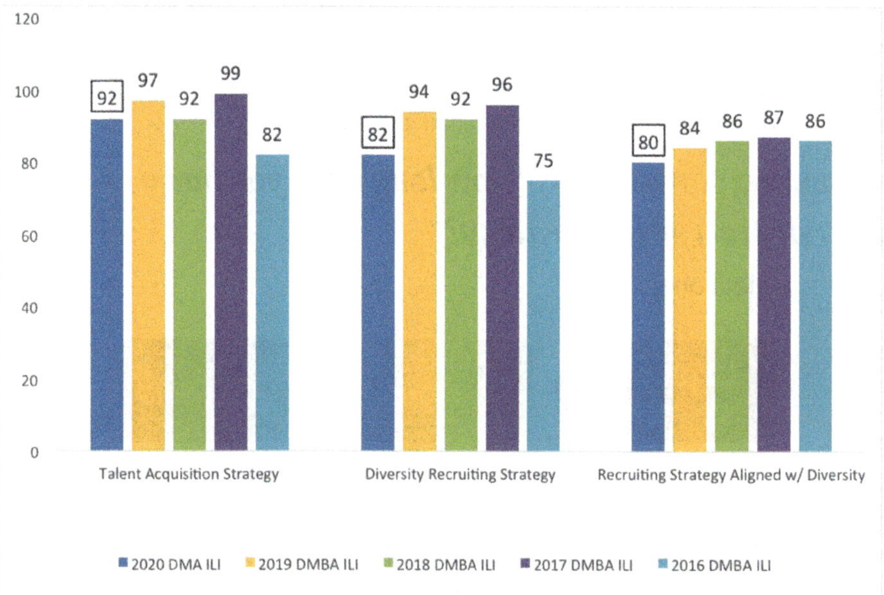

Illustration: This chart illustrates the percent of companies moving toward talent acquisition and diversity strategy alignment of goals and initiatives. Those who are implementing multiple strategies for each business segment and ensuring alignment occurs across the enterprise are undertaking another monumental task. Moreover, do not assume every company knows that each area requires its own strategy. In 2020, 92 percent of companies had a formally defined talent acquisition strategy, while only 82 percent had a diversity recruiting strategy. Of those with both, most/the overwhelming majority/only 80 percent displayed alignment between the talent acquisition and diversity recruiting strategies.

I decided to take a view to learn what some of the foundational methods companies are employing when creating organizational strategies.

Take a lesson: I know strategy is essential and should be aligned across business units with goals that are flexible and subject to adjustment. According to the DMBA Inclusive Leadership Index (ILI):

- ✓ In 2020 — 92 percent of companies have a talent acquisition strategy. This is up 10 percent since 2016. This is incredible marketplace progress to have a strategy focused on hiring talent.
- ✓ In 2020 — 82 percent of companies have a diversity recruiting strategy; up seven percent since 2016. This represents a rise of companies intentionally hiring women and people of color.
- ✓ During the period from 2016-2020, companies have gotten better at developing intentional and specific strategies for recruiting diverse talent

What this tells us:

Insight: Some of the shift in increase is due to an increased number of companies participating in the ILI in addition to the marketplace shift in recognizing the importance of multidimensional talent and recruiting strategies.

Insight: The key opportunity here is for companies to ensure each strategy is aligned to accountability with goals cascaded to each hiring manager.

We asked companies, *"How long have you had a diversity recruiting strategy?"*

✓ **select one**

The good news is that companies have been on the diversity and inclusion journey since the '90s: 75 percent of companies selected 10-plus years. With over a decade of learning from trial and error, these companies have had all the experiences that allowed them to develop practices that ultimately have become the best and leading practices today.

In jumping to the companies that have more recently implemented their inclusive diversity strategies — those who selected 5-7 years or 3-5 years — they benefit from the best practices of companies that have been on the journey more than a decade by being able to immediately implement best and leading practices. This is one of the great benefits of benchmarking and best practices.

Capturing best practices is a good thing as it allows us to learn from the mishaps other companies make. People often discuss next practices, but when it comes to recruiting, the reality is not to fix something that is not broken. We just need to build upon it. Learn from the mistakes of others and see them as opportunities to thoroughly examine and better your own practices. Be honest with yourself and identify your weaknesses that will allow you to address barriers and/or obstacles

Roadmap to Alignment

The following section will provide you with a roadmap for building a plan to align your diversity recruiting goals with your talent acquisition strategies. This model will provide you the evidence-based knowledge of best practices to help you convince upper management to move away from traditional strategies and implement a more practical and effective plan

It is important to understand the benefit of using a roadmap. It will allow you to develop your own goals and then align them with your overall strategic objectives. The processes identified below are examples taken from companies that have participated in the research and how they use the practices from our research and our index to establish their roadmaps as they venture into creating a robust best practice.

Identifying the team:

It is important to identify your team so that their role is clearly defined and the team understands the impact of their contributions.

- ˜Determining goals together with diversity, business, and talent acquisition teams who meet monthly to evaluate progress.
- Leveraging Employee Resource Groups (ERGs) for support on campus recruiting and career fairs.
- Recruiting strategy aligned with global talent recruitment team; they work directly with business teams to identify qualified talent.

Establishing metric-based goals:

Creating key performance indicators (KPIs) is a metric that helps define the activities to achieve the goals.

- Example: Xerox: The Wilson rule introduced by President Obama requires that women and minorities be among the final pool of qualified candidates for open-level management and senior-level positions

- Hiring managers should have established metrics for hiring diverse candidates. Leveraging scorecards to manage targets is one of the most popular tools used today.
- Implementing and tracking campus diversity metrics; diverse club events; career training, coaching, and counseling.
- Requiring recruiters to provide diverse slates for every open position (as the geography identifies).
- Recruiting from specific ethnic-identified colleges.
- Developing plans together to ensure same goals to achieve same outcomes; teams come up enterprise-wide programs, techniques, and tools to test new and innovative ways to fulfill hiring goals.
- Aligning your strategies with demographics for talent in the targeted communities.

Establishing your process while integrating existing systems:
Determining what steps to take to develop your process is what will help you integrate the initiatives.

- Implementing process to systemically leverage ERGs as a source for diverse talent.
- Analyzing diverse churn of hires within first year at 90 days, six months, and 12 months.
- Tracking executive and management candidates on a quarterly basis to share with leadership.
- Coordinating specific efforts for targeted recruiting of veterans, LGBTQ Plus Pronoun, and persons with disabilities.
- Using job boards for targeting diversity and identity recruiting.

Planning proven activities that yield results:
Identifying initiatives and activities that have resulted in success is important to build upon to establish your best practices.

- Increasing strategic presence at national conferences to showcase your brand and to engage in targeted diverse leadership recruiting.
- Leveraging diverse organizations that promote diversity and inclusion.
- Increasing advertising and web presence for targeted diversity sites.
- Partnering with campus diversity organizations for employment branding opportunities.
- Creating a formalized referral pool that is compensated for diverse talent.

Selecting partners who will execute your goals:
Ensuring partners are qualified to support your efforts in achieving your targeted outcomes.

- Ensuring 100 percent of retained search firms present a diverse slate for every position.
- Increasing use of boutique search firms who focus on diversity recruiting.
- Strategically leveraging professional organizations to provide a pool of diverse professional candidates.
- Engaging employees with diversity recruiting (internal partners).
- Brokering partnerships among diverse organizations for economy of scale.

Align accountability with Recruiters and Hiring Managers:

- Develop Key Performance Indicators (KPIs) that are on performance plans for both recruiters and hiring managers, not just at the enterprise-level.
- If scorecards are used, ensure the same goals for diversity hiring are used for talent acquisition and for hiring managers.
- The most effective accountability platform is ensuring diverse slates are implemented with an aligned reward system.
- Goals should be cascaded throughout the organization. Include diverse hiring metrics in individual performance plans in addition to managers and business units.
- Track external diverse hiring management along with overall hiring. Review internal talent development across the enterprise.
- Implement a high-touch, multipronged approach to identify candidates. Then establish measurable outputs with accountability to ensure diverse slates for all management positions. This will support your efforts to achieve your representation goals.
- Leverage digital campaigns, campus recruitment, ERGs, Referral Recruiting Process (RRP), and the use of diversity recruitment sites.
- Build partnerships internally and externally with metrics assigned that align with targeted acquisition goals.
- Measure applicant and acquisition demographics to measure progress. Track all dimensions of diversity: women, people of color, veterans, people with disabilities, etc.

Best Practices in Building the Plan

1 Ensure the Diversity Recruiting strategy is part of the overall business strategy.

2 Establish an inclusive task force or team that represents diversity, business, and talent acquisition functions.

3 Have diversity recruiting goals align with each function with metrics.

4 Create a process that allows for frequent review of progress.

5 Leverage employee resource groups to identify diverse and targeted groups for hiring.

6 Ensure executive alignment and accountability to diversity goals by function.

7 Leverage partnerships to achieve goals by ensuring the partners' activities are measurable for effectiveness.

8 Require accountability for diverse slates for both retained search firms and boutique minority firms.

9 Require recruiters and hiring managers to have diverse slates for all open management positions.

10 Have a consistent plan for targeted recruiting that attracts each underrepresented group.

Best Practices Toolkit: Building your Best Practices

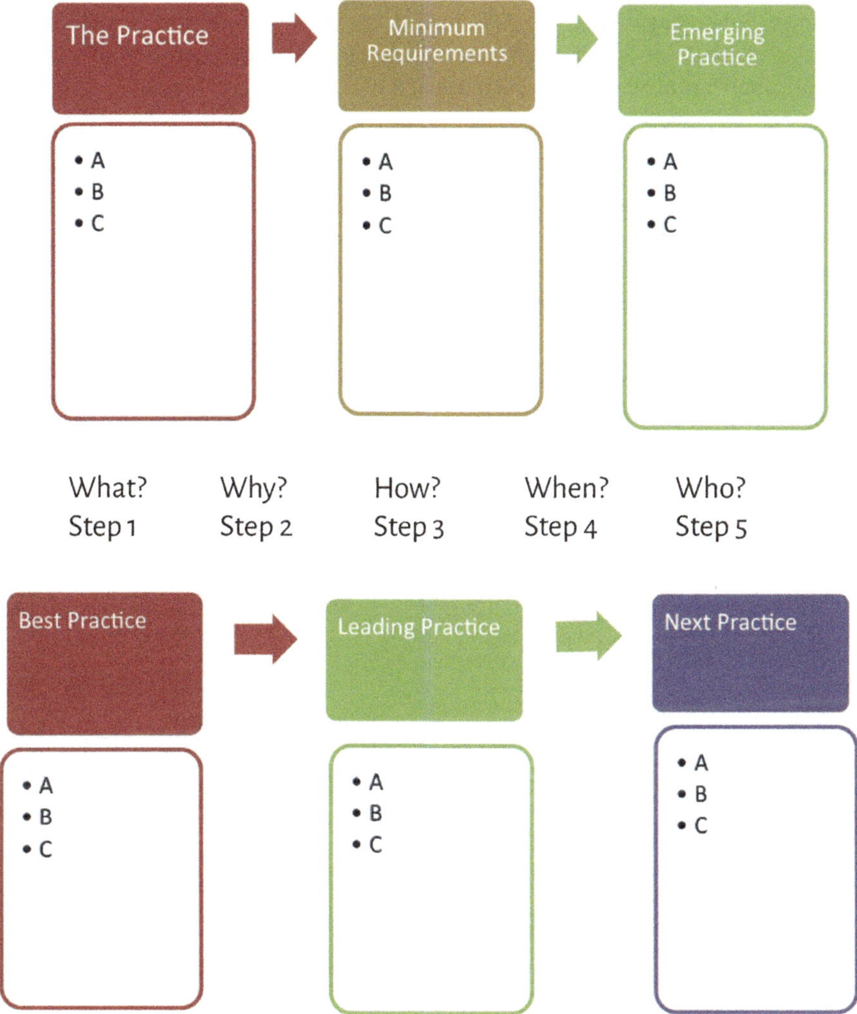

Processes are steps you should take to get work done. How work gets done is most important if it is efficient, productive, and achieves the expected outcome.

Key performance indicators (KPIs) are metrics that support identifying methods that work and those that may need attention. KPIs allow you to adjust the direction of your strategy if you get off track when achieving goals. This is when identifying best practices becomes very helpful.

Best practices are those repeatable processes that yield excellent results time and time again. They allow you to adjust the methods to uniquely fit your process.

Exercise: This exercise will allow you to work through building a best practice model. To start, you need to understand the stages of how practices are identified and/or developed.

Providing accommodations is a practice required for persons with disabilities.

Minimum requirement is what the ADA *requires* companies to offer to all people with disabilities. (Note: There is a complex issue with getting persons with invisible disabilities to disclose upon hiring that will be covered in more detail in chapter four.)

Creating a hiring process that allows people with an invisible disability to disclose and ask for an accommodation is considered an emerging practice.

Creating a safe environment for disclosure that respects and enforces an individual's right to privacy of health information while simultaneously enabling the provision of required accommodations can lead to persons with disabilities feeling secure in disclosing every time they are hired; this then becomes a best practice.

As the results continue to improve and others benefit, it may become a leading practice, especially if it is not yet prevalent in the market. Also note that next practices occur when they are innovative and new to the market.

Chapter Two

the business case for the plan: where is the talent?

"...business is going to change more in the next 10 years than it has in the last 50."
–Bill Gates

Honestly, it comes down to simple math when you think about the business case for recruiting diverse talent and spending resources to find that diverse talent. The question is, why do we have to have a business case for recruiting diverse talent? The simple answer is that we have an ever-changing population with dynamic demographics inclusive of all dimensions of diversity. With pace of change in business, we need the right talent that is inclusive of everyone.

Who is this business case for? This is not a rhetorical question; it is a real one. Companies and organizations that are new to the diversity and inclusion journey need this framework to understand how to leverage their competitive advantage. There are certain industries that have experienced phenomenal marketplace success and have been equally successful in their homogenous cultures (that is, cultures without diversity of culture, ethnicity, and gender). Popular industries like technology, manufacturing, and telecommunications, to name a few.

Mature companies that are seeking to institutionalize diversity and inclusion within their cultures require a facelift. For them, the business case for diversity recruiting continues to be relevant. I do acknowledge that mature companies are trying to fill the diverse talent gap that they have left lingering for decades. The urgency to replace diverse talent has never been a major priority since the 1980s; but today, that urgency has shifted primarily due to the changing population demographics and shrinking talent pool; some say, "The browning of younger America," ...A topic for another day.

Understanding the Impact of Population Dynamics on Workforce

The reality is that I cannot talk about the workforce without discussing the population. My premise is based on what is occurring now in 2020 and will be absolute by 2030. There are two leading organizations I trust as my data source on US population demographics; they are the United States Census Bureau and Nielsen.

The United States Census Bureau is becoming more and more adept at segmenting the population. They are the godfather of the population framework, which means it is not real until they publish it. Although the US census primarily focuses on gender, age, and ethnicity segmentation, the data does provide insights on strong population shifts and dynamics. The US census now recognizes people that identify their ethnicity as two plus races and/or multiracial; and millennials in the workforce. The US census has always tracked persons with disabilities and veterans. The good news is that the census is making progress in identifying the population dimensions.

Nielsen, on the other hand, captures data on consumer behavior across all the dimensions of diversity. Nielsen's mining of data provides the marketplace with different perspectives on workforce behaviors by understanding the social consumer behavior patterns of each group. While most companies primarily use Nielsen for business decisions on gaining competitive advantages, Diversity MBA Media leverages this data to support an enhanced understanding of social behavior and how the people, as consumers, behave as employees.

Nielsen and Diversity MBA Media have presented data together for the past several years, and it is clear to me that people do not sway far from what they do socially to what they do professionally, which means these social habits come to work. Nielsen provides us an edge in understanding the different groups so we can optimize their talents in the workplace.

Let us briefly examine what is going on in the population as compared to the workforce. The Diversity MBA Inclusive Leadership Index (referred to as DMBA ILI henceforth) shows that companies that participate in the DMBA ILI have a balanced workforce. However, the 2016 US census illustrates that when you look at the total number of Americans employed, 60 percent are white and 40 percent are people of color. It is important to note that the US census categorizes Middle Easterners as White, which does skew the workforce data for White Americans.

We asked companies, *"How many US employees are in your workforce, and what are their identities?"*

- ✓ **How many?**

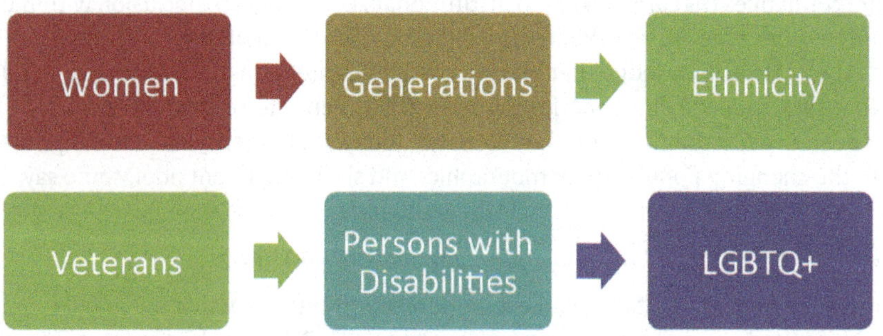

Companies track their workforce primarily for representation purposes. For federally contracted companies and organizations, they track this data as required by law. Companies are also required to track data for EEO requirements for labor laws.

While diversity is primary to ensure cultural mixes in their workforce, today it is a business necessity that inclusion is occurring simultaneously. Companies are partnering with these diverse organizations to recruit all the dimensions of diversity. I ask about the dimensions of diversity beyond ethnicity to gage how companies are tracking their workforce. It is challenging because not every employee believes it is in their best interest to identify. The job of the recruiter and hiring manager has expanded needs to solidify the cultural norms that exist in their workplace to ensure that new hires and existing employees want to identify.

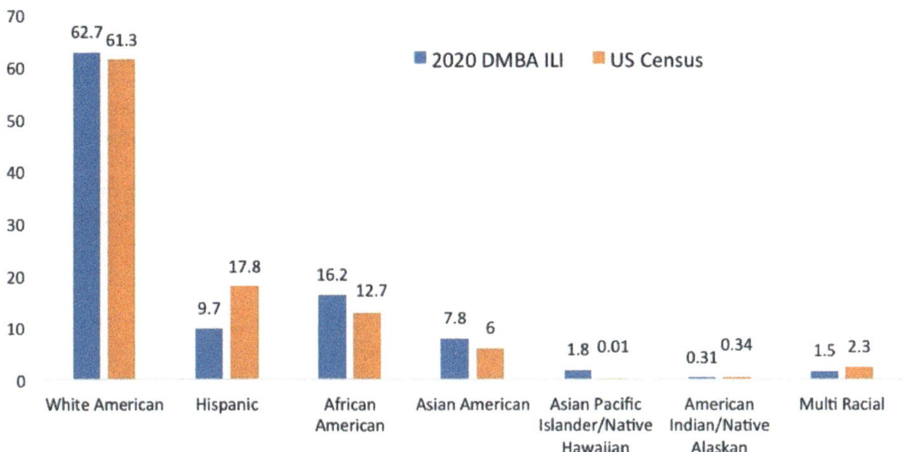

Illustration: White Americans continue to be the largest group in the workforce according to the 2016 US Census. The good news is that the percentage of White Americans is shrinking in the workforce while all the dimensions of diversity are increasing. The US Census is expanding the ethnic dimensions to be inclusive. Based on the DMBA ILI, here are some of the insights:

- 48 percent of the workforce are women, of which 70 percent are white women.
- Healthcare, Retail, Financial Services, and Education have a disproportionate number of women in the workforce with on average 68 percent; the expectation is that women are in key roles in the organization.
- Although the employee base of DMBA ILI participating companies is made up of 49 percent people of color, less than 28 percent of people of color are in management positions.
- DMBA ILI companies tend to blend all Asian groups excluding Pacific Islanders. The Asian growth population in the workforce is skewed because it includes Indians who identify as Asians.
- US Census segments Asians by country of origin, (i.e., Chinese, Indians, Filipinos, Koreans, Vietnamese, Japanese, etc.) Asian Americans typically identify as White Americans only if they are of mixed race.

Growth in Population by Race & Ethnicity

Percent of Employee Base: Population Insights from Nielsen

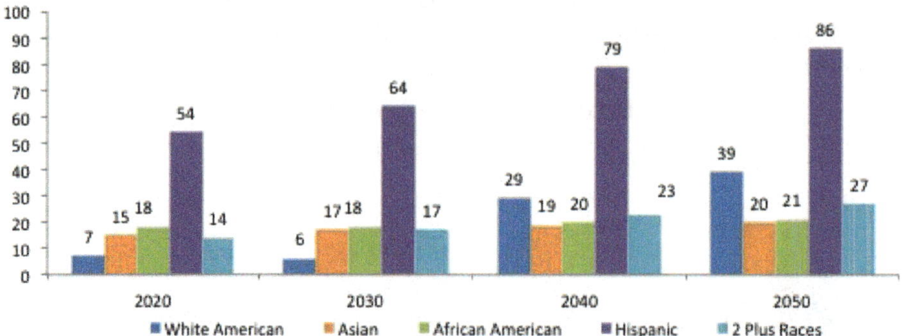

Illustration: The insights from this illustration are from Nielsen's examination of the impact of the multicultural consumer on the business. Nielsen's research also tells us where the fastest growing areas are for people of color.

- 92 percent of the total growth in the United States population from 2000 to 2014 came from multicultural consumers.
- The reality of a multicultural future is confirmed by the most populated counties in the U.S. For example, 21 of the 25 most populated counties are majority multicultural populations.
- This multicultural population is transforming the mainstream with $3.4 trillion in combined buying power.
- As demonstrated by Nielsen, the multicultural consumer is the business case for companies to ensure diversity and inclusion is an integral part of all business.
- While it appears a lot of the hype has been around 2050, Nielsen clearly illustrates that the time is now. Predictive analytics tell us that in 2020, we are well behind full workforce integration.

The importance of my sharing this data is to level set expectations and to provide you with a realistic framework for developing your strategy. For more insights from Nielsen, refer to: www.nielsen.diverseintelligenceseries.com.

The last segment I want to examine is what the existing workforce looks like from all dimensions of diversity.

It is far from acceptable that companies have thrived for decades and do not know who is in their workforce. Of course, they have a handle on gender and ethnicity. In fact, companies are getting better with ethnicity with support from the US Census. However, *identity* is still a fear factor that exists both inside companies and external to them. Recruiters are only getting partial truths because of the inherent fear these groups have with full disclosure and self-identification.

Let's examine who is in the workforce today

US Employee Base Trends by Gender & Identity

Percent of Employee Base

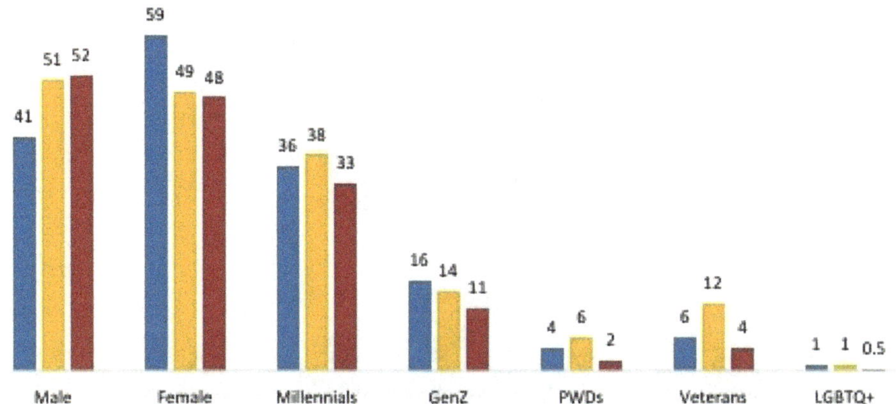

Illustration: According to the DMBA ILI, in 2020 companies have 59 percent of females and 41 percent of males among their employee bases. Millennials make up 36 percent of the workforce in the DMBA ILI. Moreover, according to the US Census, 44 percent of millennials are in the workforce. As a practice and in accordance with Equal Employment Opportunity (EEO) and Federal contractor guidelines, companies track gender, age, and ethnicity. Companies are not required to track identity dimensions other than providing services to enable employees to perform their work.

- Today, companies are focused on creating more inclusive environments for belonging. With that said, employee resource groups have become a cultural imperative to uncover personal distinctions of self-identification and full disclosure.
- The marketplace focus on Veteran initiatives supports self-identify and full disclosure in the workplace. DMBA ILI companies show 12 percent of veterans in the workplace have self-identified. Industries that are nontraditional for women (such as technology, transportation, and manufacturing to name a few) employ a higher number of veterans.
- Although persons with disabilities are the largest minority group, only 13 percent are known in the employee base. This is primarily due to the legal requirement for companies to provide accommodations. In 2019, there was a nine percent decline in self-identification from 2017.
- Within the past five years, it has been becoming safer for people of LGBTQ Plus Pronoun orientation within the workplace to identify and provide full disclosure. With less than two percent LGBTQ Plus Pronoun identified in the workforce, it is apparent that obstacles and barriers still need to be minimized, and in most organizations, addressed.

The Business Case: Diversity Recruiting to Close the Gap

Ask yourself this: If the population is browning, then why doesn't our workforce reflect it? How can I reasonably believe I cannot find talent among all groups of color? The answer lies ahead.

Components required to develop the business case framework:

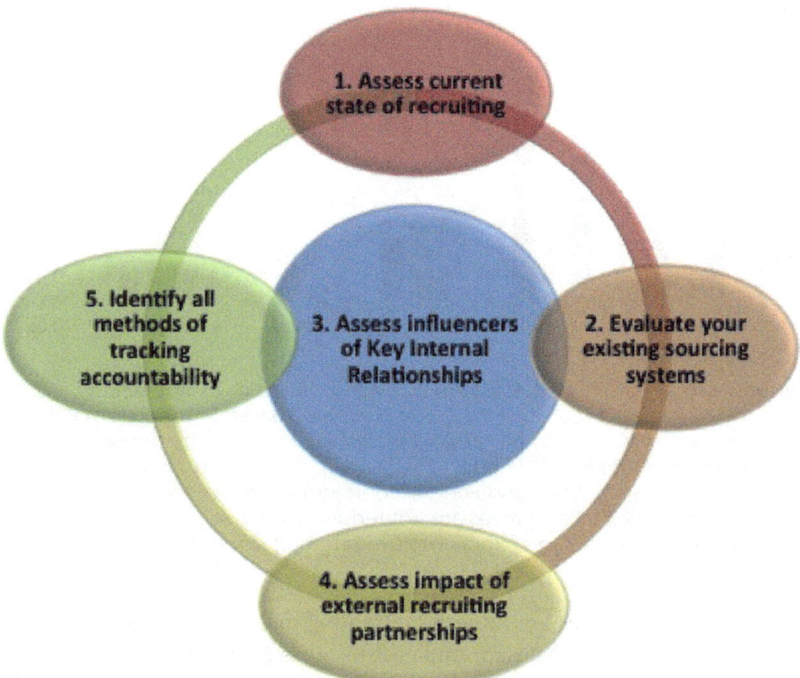

Illustration: Five strategic components to consider when developing your business framework. Once you have identified all the key areas to assess, begin to evaluate and review each component to ensure that you leverage a practical process to develop the business case for diverse talent recruiting. While I understand that development and advancement is subsequent to representation, you must first have access to a pipeline of diverse talent before anything gets started.

Consider the following when developing your five components:

1) Assess current state of recruiting – It is important to identify exactly what you have achieved and what your gaps are. Identify your barriers and/or obstacles to achieving your goals. Be sure to include human capital and budget resources in your assessment of current state.

2) Evaluate your existing sourcing system – The most common issue with the existing platforms is the decentralization of information collected. Talent matrix systems are typically only leveraged by the HR function. Understand who gets the data and how is it is shared.

3) Assess influencers of key internal relationships – Who is on the team that supports integrating the diversity strategy? Have your established functional diversity councils to support accountability?
4) Assess impact of external recruiting partnerships – External partners act as talent pools to support sourcing efforts. It is important to ensure these partners understand the outcomes desired to achieve your goals.
5) Identify all methods of tracking accountability – The ability to measure effectiveness and progress is necessary. Developing simple Key Performance Indicators (KPIs) that can be used across the enterprise provides alignment in tracking goals and identify gaps.

Business Case Format

Identify Problem

What is the problem you are trying to solve?
What is the opportunity?

Solution

How can we address the problem or take advantage of the business opportunity?

Approach

What are the viable options available for implementing the solution?

Risk Assessment

What are the risks associated with each option?
What is the cost of doing nothing?

Value Analysis

What business value is generated from each option?

Investment

Capture the cost of the activities and the return of the outcomes. What is the ROI?

The above illustration is a roadmap for developing a practical business case. It is important to tactically think through the steps of what you want to accomplish. Believe it or not, diversity recruiting deserves its own think tank. The days of putting the blame on external organizations for a company's own broken systems and embedded biases are gone. Complete the hyper-solution exercise at the end of this chapter. The hyper-solution exercise is designed to get you to the gut solution quickly, which positions you to think through one key issue at a time.

Later, my case study will illustrate how you can take your organization through this process and validate what you are doing well and acknowledge the work that still needs to be done. Basically, the paradigm shift is upon us. It is time to change.

Where is the talent?

Diverse talent can be found where population density of diversity exists. The below charts illustrate where population growth is occurring for Hispanic and other diverse populations.

The Increasingly Diverse Population of the United States

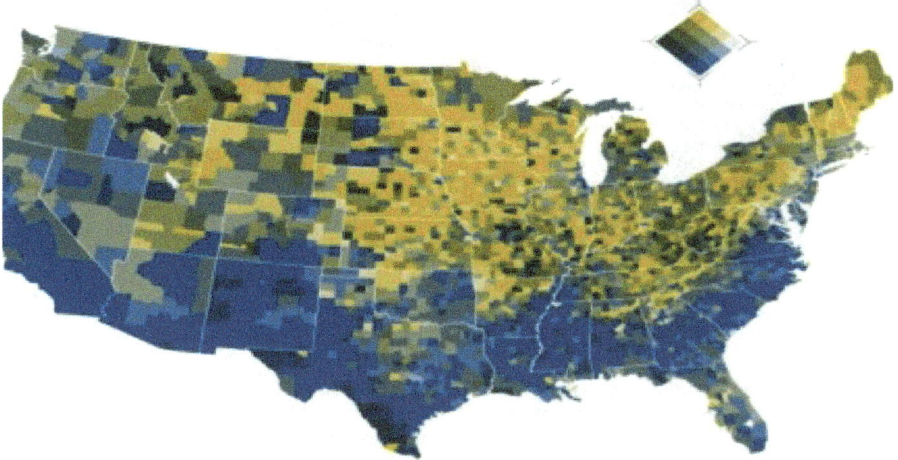

Source: Dan Keating and Laris Karklis; Nov.25,2016

Illustration: The country is becoming more diverse every year. Yellow represents low initial diversity, with big increase; **Blue** represents high diversity, with little change; **Light blue** represents low diversity, with little change; and gray also represents low initial diversity, with big increase.

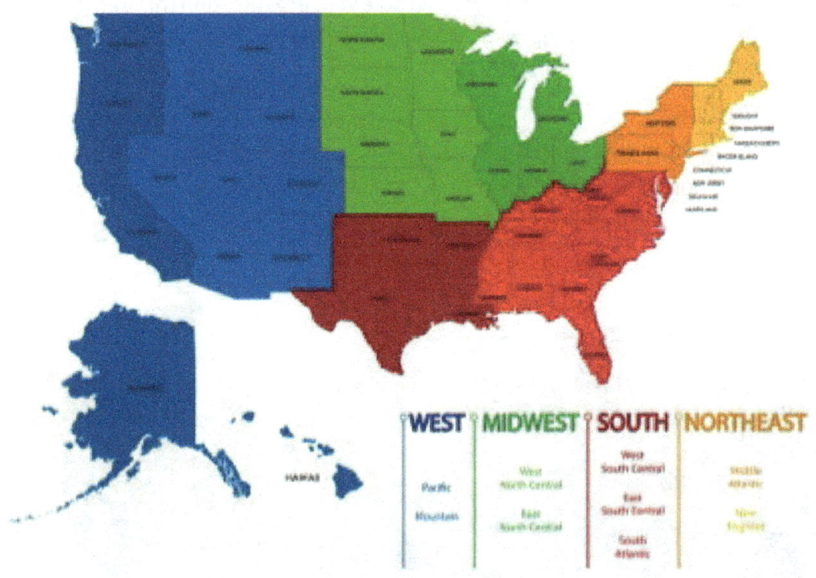

Source: US Census

Illustration: The reality is that the highest density of people of color is located in the south, northeast and some parts of the western region and Hawaii. The midwest, Alaska, and the northwest (does not appear on the map) are dominated by White Americans.

LinkedIn studies reveal that if you seek talent in locations that have a population density of certain ethnicities, organizations can build diverse pipelines and hence a diversified workforce. It is imperative that recruiters stop trying to force the fit to their recruiting models when the diversity is just not available and, therefore, the diverse talent is not available. For example, if your organization is seeking African American engineers for your operation in rural Nebraska, you cannot launch an effective or successful recruiting campaign in a state that has a population of less than five percent African Americans.

To encourage people of color to move to remote locations that require their talent but do not offer cultural inclusion, the talent search must be intentional and attractive with a career advancement plan attached to it. The reality is that talent acquisition must revisit how it arms its recruiters to engage and attract diverse talent. This is part of the PROBLEM.

20 Minute: Hyper-Solution: Identify Tools and Opportunities

Issue Statement Example: Our organization needs to do a better job aligning diverse hiring goals with talent acquisition and business functions.

Zoom Group Number:	Meeting Date	Dollar Amount or loss impact of Talent	Is This a Priority or Non-Priority Issue for you?
▪ .One or two sentences that gets to the heart of the issue or opportunity	**The Issue/Opportunity Is:**		
▪ Why is this important from your perspective?	**It Is Significant Because:**		
▪ What I really want to happen is to have a workforce that represents our community.	**My Ideal Outcome Is:**		
▪ Short bullet points that identify: • Who the stakeholders?? • The forces at work. • Today's focus. • Future impact.	**Insights and Questions from the Group Discussion**		
▪ All the various action steps that could be considered:	**Key Action(s) to Consider: Share at least one:**		

building a best-in-class recruiting engine

Part II

Chapter Three

who is doing the recruiting?

"Right time, Right Place, Right People equals Success."
–Idries Shah

The intention of this section is to provide a practical view of who is doing the recruiting; what real effort or intention looks like; and what resources are being leveraged to hire the best and brightest diverse talent. I know that when you talk about inclusive diversity, representation is not the end-all; inclusive diversity is about the mix of people in your workforce.

Does your organization have a gender, age, generation, and ethnically balanced recruiting team? Do your recruiters bring their culture and experiences to work, which may have some impact on how they make decisions? Are your recruiters working with limited resources, thereby being forced to make decisions in a vacuum? And finally, have you limited your recruiters with bare-minimum tools that eliminate the human factor? If you answered yes to any of these questions, then consider rethinking your approach, reskilling your recruiters, and reworking your plan.

Does this mean your current strategy requires disruption? It absolutely does. According to the DMBA ILI, 54 percent of companies focus on diversity recruiting, with less than 20 percent of recruiters' time is spent on diversity recruiting. In fact, when you ask the recruiters personally how they segment their time, they say they do not, it is all blended together. In fact, they capture diversity recruiting when they are at diversity events and leveraging diversity sites for online sourcing. The reality is that everyone is using the same basic platform. I must ask: How is that working for you?

The job of the recruiter is difficult if done right. It is not coincidental for recruiters to be at the right place at the right time to hire the right person. It requires intention and tactical planning with the right advocates and resources for support.

✓ **We asked companies to tell us about their sourcing teams and/or recruiters.**

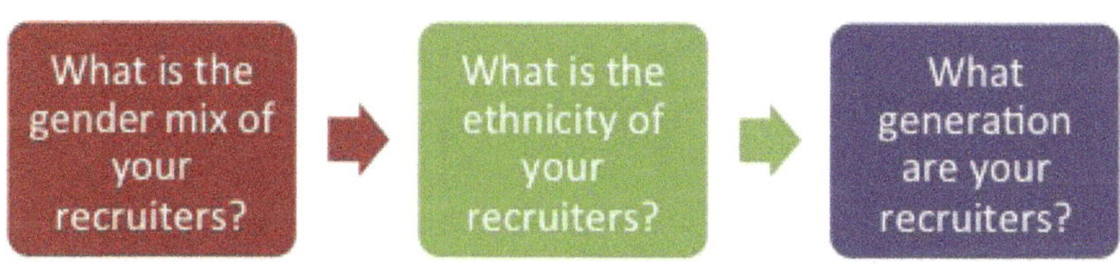

These questions allowed us to gather insights on who is doing the actual recruiting. The first responders, the first on the scene, the first to form a perception, the first to determine the fit. Generationally, across industries, recruiters are balanced.

Typically, organizations do not assess who is doing the recruiting as often as they assess the results of the recruiting efforts. To find the right people, you must have the right people looking for the talent for the role you want to fill. Has the recruiting effort become so mundane because of the internet and the absence of personal connection? At the end of the day, it is people recruiting people. Absent the human factor, and there will inherently be some misses.

The opportunity is to balance the total recruiting effort. Rework how you engage. A Best Practice is that if your recruiting team is not diverse, create expanded sourcing teams leveraging hiring managers of various culturally ethnic backgrounds.

The illustrations that follow take a detailed look at trends in the composition of sourcing teams. Several metrics are broken down in the charts, including ethnicity, gender, and age. Compare your company to the trends that are represented in the index charts below.

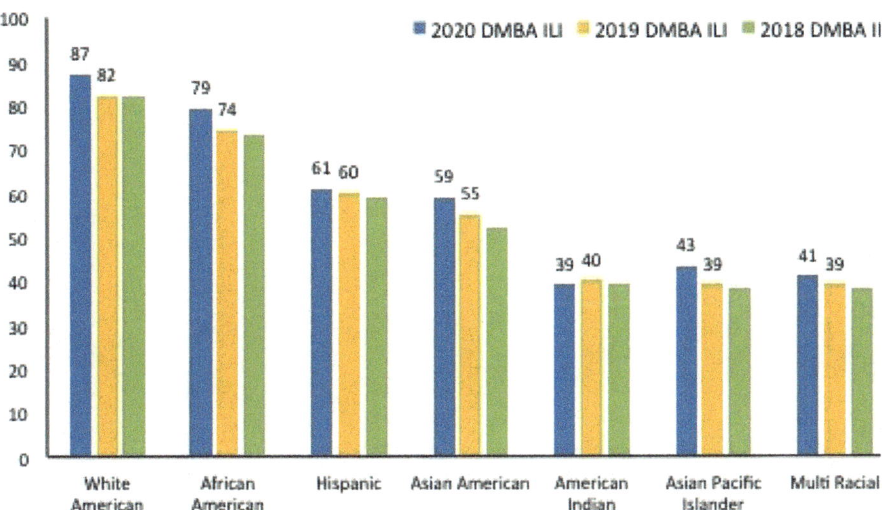

Illustration: In 2020, 87 percent of companies have White American recruiters; 79 percent of companies have African American recruiters; 61 percent of companies have Hispanic recruiters, and 59 percent of companies have Asian recruiters. These numbers illustrate that there is diversity in the recruiter ranks across industries with a moderate increase in each group from 2019. However, the reality is that 87 percent of recruiters are White American with 63 percent being women; less than 30 percent of recruiters are people of color.

There is not a best practice mix for diversification of recruiters, particularly since more than 80 percent are White Americans and more than 60 percent are White female, according to the DMBA ILI; however, to ensure recruiters have a broadened perspective to mitigate any bias in selection diversity training is imperative.

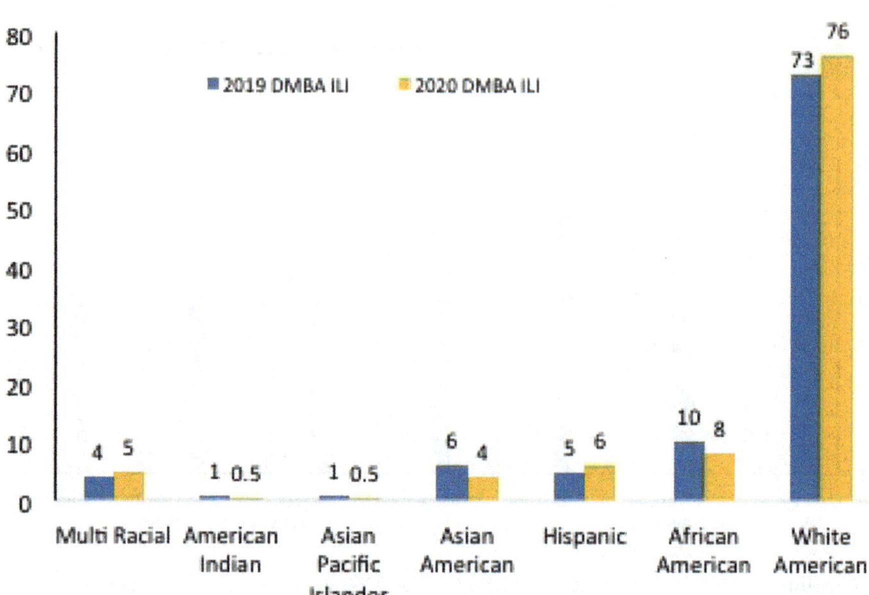

Illustration: I found a better mix of the age and gender of recruiters among companies participating in the index. I also noticed industry trends in who is doing the recruiting. It does make sense for industries that have predominantly women in their workforce to have predominantly female recruiters. The issue is this: it is predominantly White women doing the recruiting though only one lens. It is like they are the first responders leveraging all their filters to make the next-step decision.

Industries that have predominantly women include: Education, Government, Healthcare, Financial Services (mostly retail banking); Retail, and Hospitality, to name a few. Interestingly, some companies within nontraditional fields for women *also* have women who are predominantly in recruiting roles. Think about technology, telecommunications, manufacturing, and transportation; industries that have careers more conducive to men but have more women recruiting. That is a gender discussion for another day.

Recruiters by Age Trends

Average Age of Recruiters
(Includes Male & Female Genders)

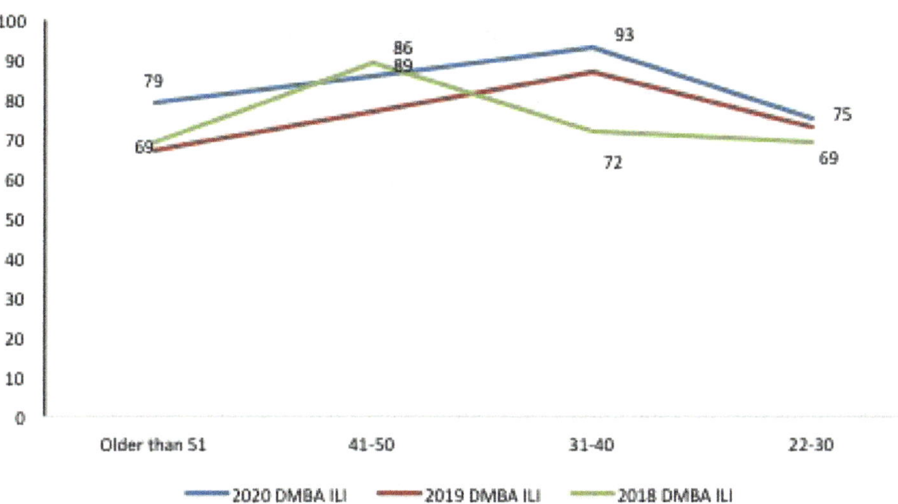

Illustration: The generation mix is on a bell curve with Boomers leveling off on the low end and Millennials and Gen Z slowly increasing on the other extreme. The middle provides the balance with Gen X and older Millennials.

I now believe it is a best practice to not only ensure your recruiting and sourcing teams are ethnically and culturally balanced, but they must, too, be generationally balanced. The experiences and perspectives of younger Millennials and Gen Zers are very different from those of us who have been in the workforce for decades. And the reality is that they will dominate the workforce by 2030.

The mere fact that the incoming generations to the workforce come with 10 times the information Boomers and Gen X had access to tells us we need to respect the foundation they bring to the workplace.

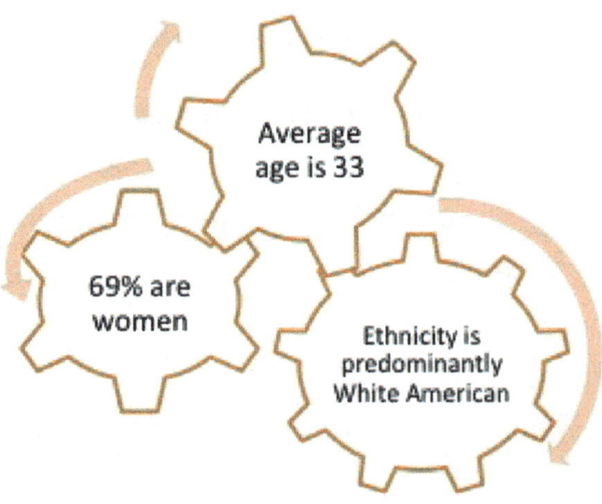

To get to the interview stage and sit across from a person is a milestone these days. There was a time when the recruiter wanted to (and needed to) sit across from the person and feel the connection. Today, the resume is working harder than ever before. The graphic below depicts a reality of... once upon a time.

Source: Google images

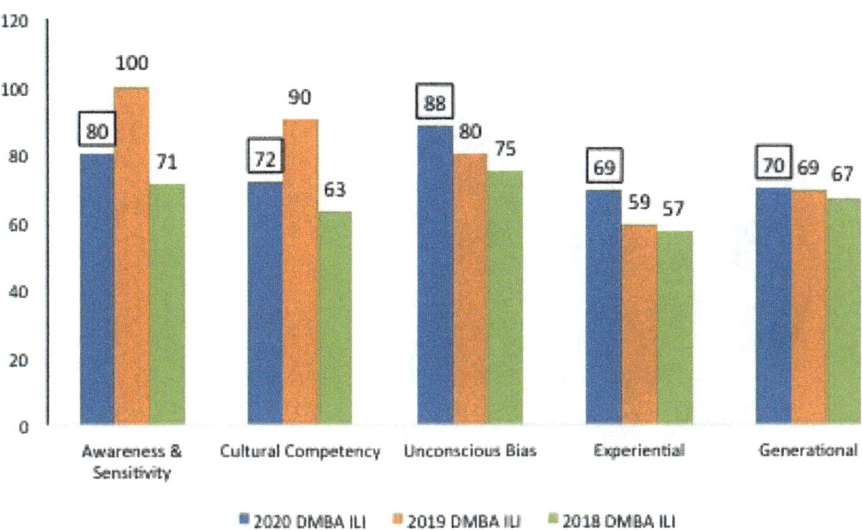

Illustration: Companies are expanding the **training** of recruiters by having them participate in both bias and cultural competency training. It is a best practice to have all recruiters, as all employees, participate in all of the dimensional diversity training. I believe the next practice is to customize this training for recruiters, especially since the majority of them are White Americans and White women.

Diversity MBA has been delivering Recruiters Boot Camp training designed to fill the gap by creating a platform for recruiters to engage in and share learnings and best practices.

Additionally, there are ways to engage recruiters in informal training that involves them in cultural experiences and provides insights on other dimensions of diversity. Employee resource groups, of course, provide experiential platforms for recruiters. And I believe that having recruiters participate in community events and initiatives broadens their perspective and helps them feel good about engaging others who are different.

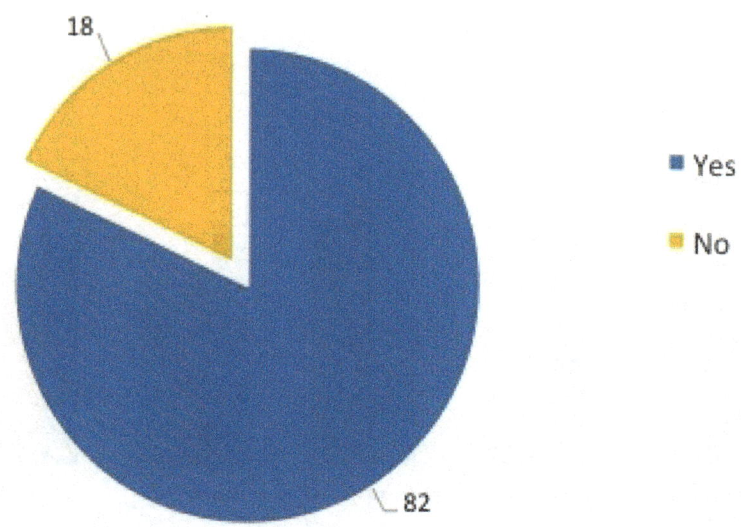

Illustration: Percentage of recruiters who are required to take diversity training. Note that recruiters spend 51 percent of their time on diversity recruiting. This data point is from companies that track the time of recruiters. Most companies blend all recruiting time and only separate it out if they have dedicated recruiters by dimension.

THE PARTNERSHIP

Each department and each person must be, without exception, on the same page. Talent acquisition, diversity & inclusion, and the business units *all* must have goals that are aligned to diversity recruitment. As well, each member from each department must have key performance metrics to manage to achieve the same outcomes.

Organizations have different models of how each department goes about achieving their goals. Below, drawing from the DMBA ILI, I have identified some of the activities to promote collaboration, intent, and motivation to drive results.

- Monthly meetings with talent acquisition and diversity & inclusion to review efforts to achieve goals.
- Diversity council members meeting with hiring managers to help them with barriers they encounter.
- Guidebooks to support managers in having tough conversations about micro-messages in hiring.

Ideal Traits for Recruiters

1 Confidence. There is a reason that the industry tends to attract extroverts.

2 Good communication skills.

3 Approachable demeanor.

4 Good listener.

5 Strong influence skills.

6 Results driven.

7 Good at multitasking.

8 Patience and empathy for others.

9 Passion for work.

10 Strong interpersonal skills.

Chapter Four

understanding bias in talent acquisition

"What gets measured gets done... What gets rewarded gets repeated!"
–John E. Jones III

Let me introduce Paul Meshanko, MBA, CSP, Founder and president of Legacy Business Cultures, and Author of The RESPECT EFFECT. I invited Paul Meshanko to join me in writing this chapter as a contributing expert, because he brings a perspective on the intersection of respect, bias and diversity that supports the discussion in mitigating bias in talent acquisition.

I sat down with Paul to interview him on the work he has been doing the past two decades and the research his team are continuing to compile. Paul's clients range from Fortune 500 companies to large government agencies, to mid-size businesses. I just had three clarifying questions for Paul. I want the readers to understand how bias influences decisions in hiring; how we as individuals can manage our own bias; and the impact of respect in creating an inclusive selection process.

Paul shared, there are two primary applications that bias applies to. The first is to help create more respectful and inclusive work cultures. We look at closely how unconscious biases can inhibit one on one respectful interactions between people and general behaviors that contribute to inclusive cultures. And secondly, how unconscious bias leads to ineffective and poor decision making relative to group and individual levels within organizations.

How do we know we are under the influence of bias? Bias is typically an unidentifiable, but distinct attraction towards a person or an aversion away from them. "I like them, or I don't like them". Either perspective can lead to poor candidate selection. In some cases when someone resonates with the interviewer, (being just like me), or like the rest of our team members, instant attraction is formulated. These cause short cuts in the thoroughness of the interview process thus leaving the potential of not uncovering problematic areas that the candidate may possess. As well as, in some cases lowering the bar for other candidates because unknowingly, we prequalify with this internal bias checklist.

On the other hand, bias can get in the way of identifying good candidates because of how it affects our liking mechanisms. For example, how people show up differently, whether its age, skin color, hair color, language accent, or how they dress, could be something the interviewer does not like, thus unintentionally raises the bar for them and in some cases does not move them through the selection process for relatively superficial reasons.

I asked, "How does your brain work in terms of understanding of how bias is manifested?" Paul explained, we have hardwired bias based on our upbringing and environment.

However, the two most proven techniques for managing bias are relatively simple: Awareness and Awareness with Concern. 1) Awareness. The more times an individual invests in understanding where their own bias is identified, the less likely this bias will creep into their decision making. The second part is Awareness with Concern. This is the best inoculation in demonstrating bias in how we recruit and interview candidates. (Recommended resource: Harvard Implicit Bias Association).

I asked, how do you connect the notion of respect in creating inclusive teams that are interdependent? Respect is about the conveying value to another person. For example, value can be as subtle as eye contact and active listening. Inclusion is about the conveyance of belonging. You cannot authentically practice inclusion without having practiced respect for that person. Once you have mastered respect in a one-on-one interaction, then the behavior of respect is telling the other person, they are valued regardless of the community they are from.

We must learn to redirect our thinking back to the critical thinking part of our brain. Specifically, the prefrontal cortex which is more logical and rational than emotional.

We asked companies, *"Do you specifically train your recruiters on unconscious bias?"*

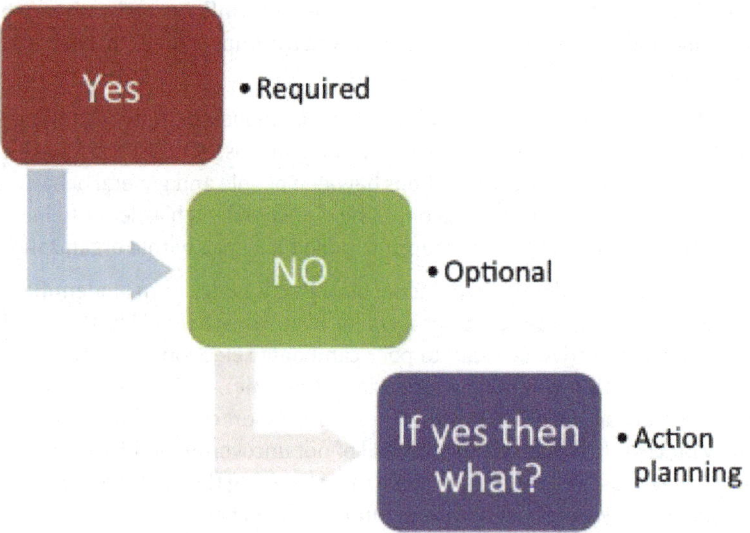

Based on the DMBA ILI, I have seen more than a 50 percent increase in bias training from 2016 (36 percent) to 2020, with 80 percent of companies training recruiters on unconscious bias in 2020. It is important to understand that recruiters require additional training as well as a separate training platform on bias, just as they have for specialized training like disability ADA legislation. It is imperative that companies recognize that recruiters are subject to systemic bias embedded in the talent acquisition process, as nothing changes until it is called out.

We asked companies, *"Do you have a process to identify systemic bias in the workplace?"*

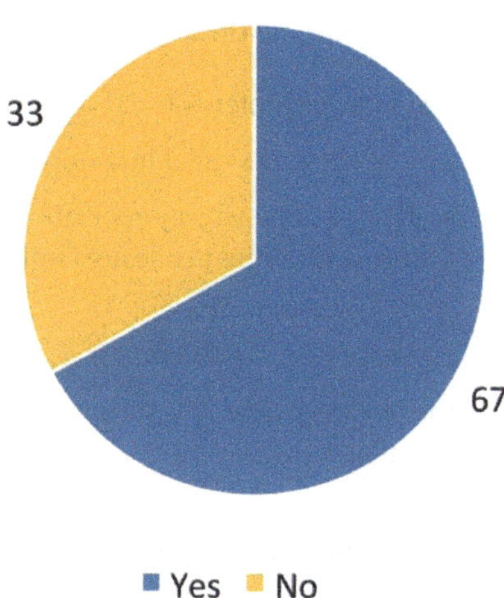

Illustration: The chart above captures the percentage of companies that have some type of system in place to identify bias through surveys, focus groups, or interviews. The important question to ask is: once bias is identified, what systems are necessary to mitigate it and change?

For recruiters, it is important to be aware that all the unconscious biases listed can impact and skew the ideal traits. For example, confidence is the belief in one's ability to do a good job. However, part of a recruiter's job is to evaluate the competency of the potential candidate. Part of a debiasing strategy is to question assumptions and to question visceral responses that may have more to do with the recruiter's implicit biases, either for an ingroup member or lack of empathy for an outgroup member.

Recognizing Unconscious Bias in the Workplace

According to Andrea Choate, Human Resource Executive, there are more than 150 types of unconscious bias that are common to the workplace. It's a business imperative to support employees with the resources to be aware of their biases, and what can be done to mitigate them.

Here are the Top 10 Most Common Unconscious Biases in the Workplace.

1. **Affinity Bias.** Having the tendency to prefer or like those like oneself.
2. **In-Group Bias.** Perceiving those who are similar in a more positive way.
3. **Halo Effect.** Having the tendency to believe only good about someone because they are liked or letting someone's positive qualities in one area influence the overall perception of that person.
4. **Out-Group Bias.** Perceiving those who are different in a more negative way.
5. **Perception Bias.** Having the tendency to form assumptions or stereotypes about certain groups thus making it impossible to make objective decisions about members of those groups.
6. **Blind Spot.** Identifying biases in others but not oneself.
7. **Confirmation Bias.** Having the tendency to seek information that confirms pre-existing beliefs or assumptions, or conversely to discount information that is incongruent with one's assumptions.
8. **Group Think.** Having the tendency to try and fit into a particular group by either mimicking their behavior or holding back on sharing thoughts and opinions out of fear of potential exclusion.
9. **Belief Bias.** Having the tendency to decide whether an argument for something is strong or weak based upon whether one agrees with the conclusion of that argument.
10. **Anchoring Bias.** Having the tendency to rely heavily upon the first piece of information available rather than seeking out and fully evaluating multiple sources of information when deciding.

Practices to Mitigate Systemic Bias in Talent Acquisition

According to the 2021 and 2020 DMBA Inclusive Leadership Index; and specific research compiled within the past decade by Dr. Suri Surinder, CEO, CTR Factor & Chief Learning Officer, Diversity Learning Solutions, organizations must conduct a comprehensive examination of their existing systems, policies, and practices to begin the identification process to mitigate systemic bias.

Below are the top areas and definitions that should be considered for review and re-design of the talent acquisition process.

1 **Analyzing**
Key Leading Indicators like diverse applications per requisition, screens per application, tests per screen, interviews per test, offers per interview, acceptances per offer, and starts per acceptance can identify drop-off points of diverse candidates in the hiring process. Examine the outcomes of each ethnic group compared to white Americans. Companies that do not have diverse slate requirements hire on average 50 percent less people of color. The DMBA ILI has 83 percent of companies with diverse slates and 56 percent of them have accountability systems in place.

2 **Sourcing**
Identify both internal and external sourcing platforms your organizations leverage on a regular basis. Compare the diverse applicant numbers to the overall applicant number from each source; then assess the rate of acceptance and loss by diverse applicants at each source. For example, if you're sourcing HBCUs and HSIs, how many students interviewed, hired, and lost as compared to white applicants from the same geographic areas. Consider internal sourcing options: Typically, 15-20% of the employees at large companies are members of Employee Resource Groups (ERG). If each ERG member could bring one hire from their network through an effective referral program, that can increase diversity by 15-20%.

3 **Screening**
Modify Position Descriptions by eliminating words and phrases that reduce response rates from diverse constituencies. Remove information from resumes regarding name, graduation dates, geographic residence, educational institutions, and other topics that might introduce unconscious bias. Do not include the job requirements in the requisition – just a description of what the role entails. Include a link to a questionnaire that has 10-15 multiple choice questions answerable in 5 min. about the education, experience, skills, knowledge, and attributes of the applicant, without requiring a resume.

4 **Qualifying**
Some organizations, like consulting companies, utilize case studies to test for problem solving and analytical skills. While this kind of testing can identify the potential of a prospective candidate's fit for specific open roles, they can also eliminate good candidates who may not be high on test-taking skills. It also does not check for critical emotional intelligence skills that might be more highly correlated to work-related success at many companies. What percentage of the candidates are Black and Hispanic that are not passing the testing qualifications? Moreover, this eliminates the underrepresented and indigenous populations.

5 **Interviewing**
Team and panel interviewing are the leading practices to mitigate systemic bias, especially since 76 percent of recruiters are white Americans and 67 percent are white women according to 2020 DMBA ILI. Simultaneous interviews with multiple interviewers on a panel ensure that everyone rates the candidate contemporaneously on a set of standardized questions. Careful selection of panelists to ensure diverse representation, coupled with training and certification of interviewers on processes to mitigate unconscious bias.

6 **Offering**
Typically, offers focus on the 3B's – Base, Bonus, Benefits – and seek to differentiate from other suitors based upon current financials or prospects. Large companies tend to have an unfair advantage in getting the best talent because of deeper pockets and more resources. To even the odds in their favor, and to play a different game than their competition, some companies are focusing on 3L's in their offer – Location, Loans, and Learning. In today's environment, pay equity audits need to occur more regularly to identify the compensation, gender, and racial bias. DMBA ILI research in 2020 has 57 percent of companies doing pay audits with only 36 percent taking corrective action.

7 **Onboarding**
New hires may not be fully aware of the unique culture of the company and what kinds of behaviors are required for success within that environment. This can lead to early missteps and misalignments that are tough to recover from and can result in early departures and stranded investment. Address the culture of the company along specific dimensions like hierarchical orientation, group orientation, communication style, task orientation and other dimensions. Assess how the individual's profile maps to the company's culture, which elements are a natural fit, and which ones may need intentional bridging. Assess the rate of churn of people of color within the first two years, (especially Black and Hispanic). If people of color are leaving at the rate of 15-20 percent within first two years, bias is embedded in the culture.

8 **Developing**

Experiential learning has become the leading way to engage employees culturally. ERGs facilitate the process for intercultural learning and development. Consider platforms that allows employees to contribute to projects in other parts of the company that build targeted skills and knowledge bases (separate from their day jobs). Offer access to low cost, text-based coaching to less tenured employees so that they have timely and consistent access to advice regarding challenges and issues they face. Retention and low churn of early hires are an integral part of the talent acquisition process.

9 **Measuring**

According to Dr. Surinder multiplicative scorecards provides more wholistic incentives. If the weights are lower than 10% for diversity, don't bother including it as an additive metric on scorecards. It won't get the attention intended. Use diversity metrics as a multiplicative metric on the scorecard, so that leaders can get more than 100% of their bonus by meeting these objectives. This focuses on the upside of making diversity targets much higher than 5% impact on bonuses. According to the DMBA ILI ,90 percent of companies use scorecards across the enterprise to ensure alignment, but it does not fix the systemic bias issues that creep into the performance by objective plans.

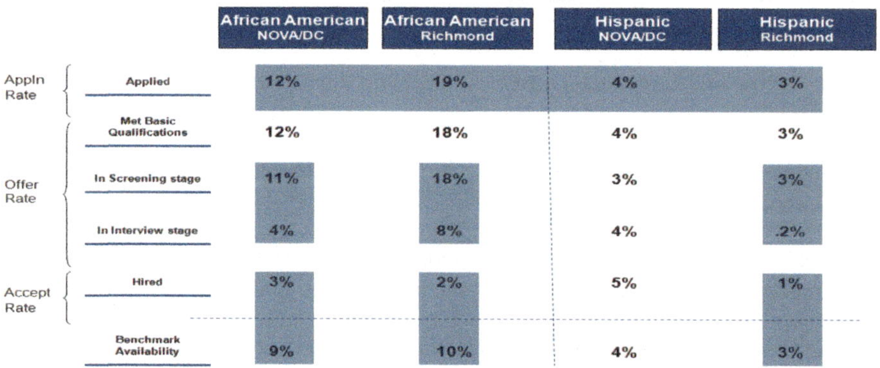

Dr. Suri Surinder examines how companies measure every element of their current state using KPIs to help identify the gaps by ethnic group. Systemic bias is embedded in the processes that are used repeatedly. Assessing what happens at each stage for each group create opportunities for improvement and process redesign. Use the steps to create your applied chart of acquisition.

Best Practices for Managing Bias in Talent Acquisition

1 Identify interview panelists in collaboration with Human Resources and Business Unit Leaders.

2 Provide an interview guide with standardized job-related and corporate value-related questions, along with guidelines and tips for follow-up questions.

3 Provide conscious and unconscious bias training to reduce rater bias; e.g., intonations, ratings, perceptions, etc.

4 Monitor the selection rate for adverse impact and the possibility of affinity or ingroup bias.

5 Implement accountability for diverse hiring at all levels with alignment among functions and human resource.

6 Establish formal diversity recruiting trainings for recruiters that include multiple levels of understanding of systemic bias and unconscious bias as recruiters.

7 Leverage Employee Resource Groups/Networks to support referral-based hiring as well as participate as part of the hiring review team.

8 Implement systems to eliminate discrimination in the job posting and resume screening.

9 Establish reward and recognition systems for teams that are creative and innovative in developing processes to reduce bias in hiring.

10 Establish a zero-tolerance policy that eliminates bias and discrimination in the talent acquisition process, once identified.

Chapter Five

resources, process & structure

"Step by step and the thing is done."
–Charles Atlas

This chapter is intended to share insights on how recruiting resources are allocated and how the process aligns with the recruiting structure. Believe it or not, diversity recruiting not only requires resources, it requires the process by which the things are organized to get done to achieve the results you intend. Is there a best-in-class structure that drives resources? ABSOLUTELY.

With the evolution of the human resource function, I must be fair and recognize that this function continues to evolve and transform. It is important to understand some fundamentals of the evolution of human resource because of its direct impact on the changes in the recruiting role. Several decades ago, the human resource function affectionately known as the *personnel department* had a business function that supported the hiring process. Then, during the 80s and 90s, the human resource function became more strategic and developed a business partner role supporting hiring managers. In the millennium, the human resource function has evolved into talent management that is all-inclusive of hiring, retaining, and advancing talent. Today, recruiters and hiring managers have a much different job when deciding if they are hiring for sustainability, diversity, or opportunity.

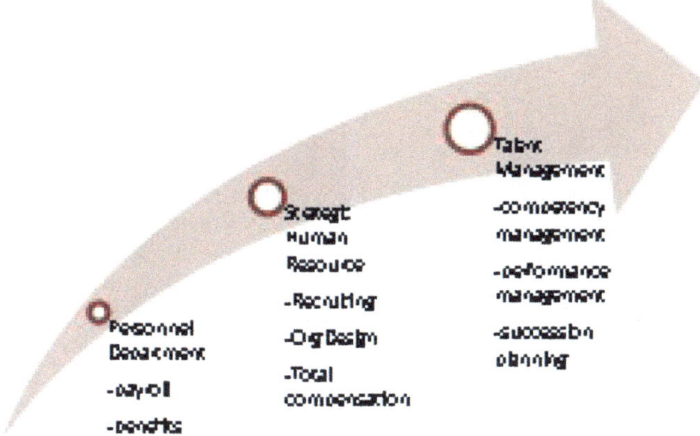

Evolution of Human Resource Function

Rev Up the Resources

Ninety percent of human resource budgets are responsible for diversity and inclusion and recruitment resources. The trend is that less than 10 percent of human resource budgets are allocated to Diversity & Inclusion and an average of 20 percent of recruiters' time is spent on diversity recruiting. Ironically, the diversity office is supposed to have an impact on the recruiting efforts, but the work is out of alignment because accountability does not exist.

What resources are necessary to build a comprehensive and successful recruiting engine? What does it take to ensure you are gaining every advantage and to be confident your recruiters are exhausting all possibilities in finding the best talent for the available opportunities? How important are the people in your company? I know, I know... *People are your most valued asset*. I hear this cliché over and over, but the proof is in the budget.

Over the past five years, I have asked a series of questions regarding budgets allocated to the human resource function, the recruiting function, and the diversity function for the purpose of understanding if there is equity in the distribution of the budget resources. The reality is that companies allocate resources based on their commitment to recruiting the best talent and their commitment to diversity.

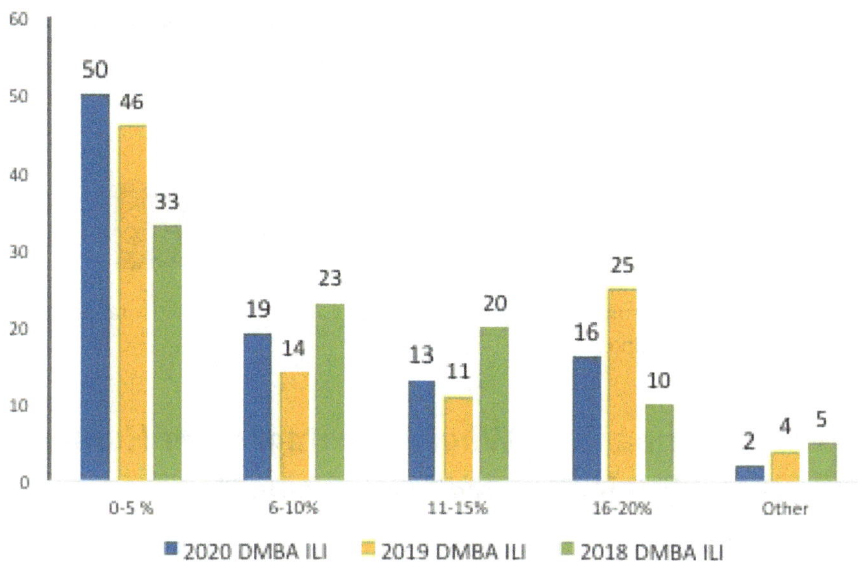

Illustration: Human Resource budget allocation as a percentage of the total company budget. This is important because it determines the investment human resources can make in talent acquisition and diversity recruiting.

Strategy requires resources to drive implementation. Most human resource budgets are allocated to managing and developing talent. I have seen a decline in the percentage of dollars allocated to Diversity & Inclusion, diversity recruiting, and talent acquisition overall.

It is imperative that diversity strategies are aligned with business strategies to ensure that the right talent is in the right positions.

Below are insights for how companies are allocating their resources to drive diversity recruiting.

We asked companies, "*What percentage of the total company budget is allocated to Human Resources?*"

- ✓ **select one**

>10% → >15% → >20%

More than 65 percent of companies declared that up to 10 percent of the total company budget is allocated to people.

We asked companies, "*What percentage of the Human Resources budget is allocated to recruiting?*"

- ✓ **select one**

>10% → >15% → >20%

More than 50 percent of companies allocate up to 15 percent of their human resources budget to recruiting talent.

We asked companies, "*What percentage of the Human Resources budget is allocated to the Diversity & Inclusion function?*"

- ✓ **select one**

>5% → >7% → >10%

More than 75 percent of companies allocate less than 10 percent of the human resource budget to the Diversity & Inclusion function. When asked if companies have a separate budget for diversity recruiting, more than 60 percent of companies do not segment the budget for diversity recruiting.

Budget Allocation Trends - Percent of Companies

Talent Acquistion | **Diversity, Equity & Inclusion**

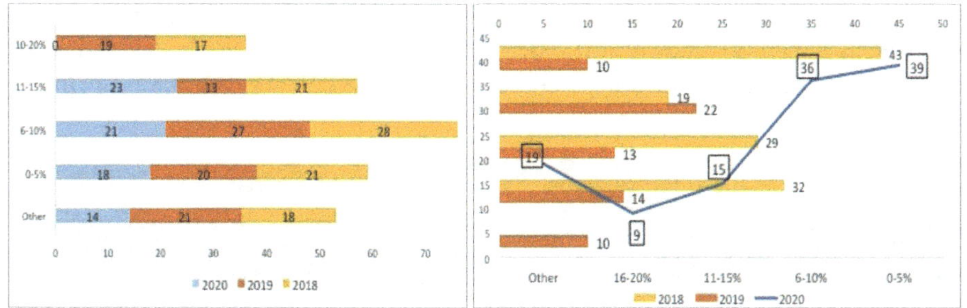

STEPS TO BEST PRACTICE PROCESS:

The components of a recruitment process should be simple. Be sure to track results because if nothing measured, nothing gained. You want to be able to know when and how you improve, as well as what can be adjusted quickly.

RECRUITMENT PROCESS STEPS

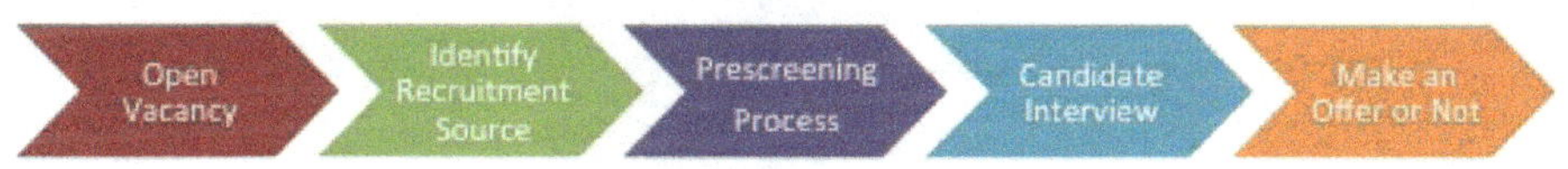

Decision Process

WHO

HR Manager	HR Team	HR Manager	Hiring Manager	Hiring Manager

OUTCOME

Job Description	Channel	Resume Selection	Final Candidate(s)	New Hire

Simple and straightforward recruitment processes deliver the best results.

TECH TOOLS

What is the best-in-class tech tools on the planet? What will allow recruiters to source and hire talent in a global marketplace? In today's competitive environment, recruiting teams must be in touch with the latest technology as well as future forecasts in how that AI will impact the hiring of talent. Developing an agile, modern, and integrated recruiting technology stack is now a top criterion for success.

Moreover, it is not enough to merely stay in the tech sourcing game; you must be ahead of it with a mindset of continuing learning. While metrics are a must, it is equally as important to have frequent reviews of the effectiveness of the tools and processes being utilized. Do not be afraid to change tools after six months of use with little to no results.

The illustration below shows what the ideal recruiting software landscape looks like. I recommend you build you own. First, assess what you have, how effective it is, and what needs to be changed. Next, review your timeline and budget; then get approval and make it happen

building a best-in-class sourcing platform

Part III

Chapter Six

in search of the mix: *recruiting diverse talent*

"If you exclude 50 percent of the talent pool, it's no wonder you find yourself in a war for talent."
–Theresa J. Whitmarsh

Part III is designed to review what companies are doing around targeted recruiting. I will examine the most popular platforms utilized for diversity and targeted recruiting with the intent to provide insights that will support the validation of your process as well as support any aha moments you may gain that will facilitate adjusting your perspective.

I hate bringing up the old cliché that companies have used for decades, "We just cannot find qualified people of color here in the United States." Oh my! I am so tired of this broken record; I just cannot stand it. The reality is not having a defined and consistent talent pool to funnel the pipeline has created a combination of things. Recruiters are under-resourced, lazy, and do not want to do the extra work; they are not serious about hiring people with differences; and/or they lack the skills. Let us not forget those hiring managers who settle for being comfortable, not necessarily hiring the best candidate but instead the most amenable candidate. I will not apologize for stating the obvious; if you find yourself getting upset, it may be that you that feel some responsibility, and that's a good thing.

Recruiters: There is not a best-practice mix for diversification of recruiters, particularly since more than 60 percent of recruiters are White American and White female. However, the lens in which recruiters source talent is as equally important as their ethnicity. Diversity MBA 50 Out Front companies have a more balanced mix of recruiters on average than the marketplace. However, I do recognize that some industries that have more women in their workforce will inherently have more women dominant in the recruiting ranks.

The opportunity lies in companies engaging ERGs and hiring managers to fill both the ethnicity and identity gap on the recruiting and hiring teams.

We asked companies, *"Who are the top five diverse organizations you have strategic relationships with for the purpose of developing an experienced diverse-hire talent pool and pipeline?"*

✓ **Select your top five organizations. The chart below illustrates the results:**

Diverse Professional Recruiting Trends

Professional Associations: Percent of Companies

Targeted Recruiting: Professional associations continue to be the preferred source for diverse professional, and experienced hire recruiting. However, in 2018 and 2019, you see the increase primarily due to companies intentionally focusing on African Americans and Hispanics. The slight decline in 2020 is due to the COVID-19 pandemic.

Moreover, I am seeing a decline in the frequency in which companies' partner with associations on a national scale. Companies are more focused on local strategies to support their targeted hiring. Our results indicate companies have more success in meeting diverse hire metrics when they engage in local targeted partnerships as compared to national partnerships.

Below are a series of charts that illustrate the three-year trend of how companies leveraged professional associations for diverse talent as their number one strategic sourcing outlet.

Diverse Professional Recruiting Trends

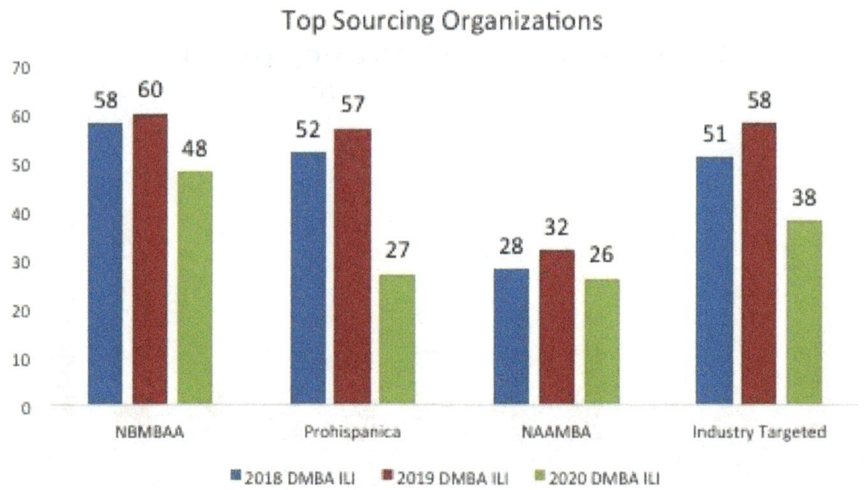

Illustration: This chart shows where companies sourced for people of color specifically. The trend was to source from professional organizations and industry-specific targeted organizations to secure both experienced hires and graduate-level talent.

When you think about it, companies invest human capital, resources, and cash into their relationships with professional associations/organizations; yet they fail to put systems and metrics in place to ensure they receive their expected outcome. Today, it is a business imperative that talent acquisition reevaluates how it leverages its tools for all targeted recruiting sourcing.

Illustration: The results on this chart indicate that in the within the past three years, companies have had fluctuating diverse hire results. I believe this is based on companies that are tracking their activity of sourcing and actual hires versus companies not having systems in place. Not long ago, companies planned with their professional association partners and shared tools to ensure they achieved their mutual goals. While I recognize that there are many competing priorities today, I do believe that to drive success, everyone must be on the same page—and that demands *accountability*.

It is a best practice to have dedicated recruiters to manage targeted sourcing. Eighty-two percent of companies have dedicated recruiters primarily for veterans, persons with disabilities, and LGBTQ Plus Pronoun. However, diverse professional sourcing tends to be embedded within general recruiting responsibilities. In 2019, with 75 percent of recruiter's time spent on diversity hiring and sourcing, my question is: Why aren't the results better?

I know that in today's competitive environment, companies need to be innovative, creative, and impactful with their programming if they want to recruit experienced talent.

- The insights below provide examples of innovative and/or impactful programming conducted jointly with professional organizations that resulted in hiring.
- Partnering with the consortium (Diversity MBA program) in their orientation program event, allowing employees to engage and make student connections that result in private interviews and hiring.
- Talent acquisition aligning a staff recruiter as a liaison to each professional organization to ensure the association/organization can fulfill the goals of the company and, together, planning events for attracting talent.
- Holding networking receptions hosted by the companies interested in

recruiting specific diverse talent from that organization/association.

- Partnering with educational institutions and associations to execute events that ensure both entities share in messaging and resources, connecting so they can reach the targeted audience.
- Talent acquisition aligning a staff recruiter as a liaison to each professional organization to ensure the association/organization can fulfill the goals of the company and, together, planning events for attracting talent.
- Holding networking receptions hosted by the companies interested in recruiting specific diverse talent from that organization/association.
- Partnering with educational institutions and associations to execute events that ensure both entities share in messaging and resources, connecting so they can reach the targeted audience.
- Case study experiences provide an experiential selection process, ensuring each candidate gains firsthand industry knowledge in addition to being exposed to interviewing and meeting a panel of experts.
- Sponsoring and hosting private events at national conferences to meet identified candidates during event.
- Management Leadership for Tomorrow is a program that provides diverse students with tools and resources to successfully enter the workforce. They also provide opportunities for professionals to receive coaching.
- Healthcare organizations align their organizations with the fellows by ensuring they have the firsthand opportunity to hire the ready talent.
- Partnering with the local chamber of commerce focused on people of color presents great opportunities for companies to source talent they normally do not see at conferences. Chambers are also able to reach industry-specific candidates.
- Leveraging employee resource groups and diversity councils allow companies to expand the hiring teams for diverse specific interviewing. Creating interview panels is an example to ensure diverse perspectives in talent selection process.
- Encouraging talent acquisition to volunteer time with organizations, helping build their recruiting strategy and plans.
- Hosting local student conferences with ALPFA has resulted in direct hiring of local Hispanic talent, in addition to meetings, receptions, etc.

Best Practices for Professional Recruiting

1. Talent acquisition must be committed to ensuring professional partnerships are aligned with goals, targets, and rewards.
2. The best practices are the repeatable activities that systematically drive processes to achieve results.
3. Talent acquisition must be engaged in real partnerships nurturing relationships and creating sustainable institutional progress.
4. Ensure hiring managers are in partnership with talent acquisition and have a dashboard to align targeted goals.
5. Establish KPIs and metrics that can measure each activity invested in the association/organization.
6. Create a process that allows for frequent review of progress with external partnerships.
7. Engage employee resource groups to participate on diverse panels and attend all recruiting events, etc.
8. Leverage partnerships to achieve goals by ensuring partner activities are measurable for effectiveness.
9. Require accountability (with identified consequence or reward) for diverse slates for both retained search firms and boutique minority firms.
10. Require recruiters and hiring managers have diverse slates for all open management positions.

Chapter Seven

hidden talent: people with disabilities (PWD)

"Count me in for my ability and let me show you the talent I can be."
–Pamela A. McElvane

Persons with disabilities make up 18.1 percent of the workforce and are the world's largest minority, which means that 15-20 percent of every country's population is persons with a disability. However, an estimated 35 percent of the US population aged 21-64 years has a disability. People are working longer and retiring later, and this has a direct impact on the growing workforce of people with disabilities. There is a both a business case and a talent case why more attention should be paid to this group. According to Nielsen, persons with disabilities is the largest consumer group, and it transcends all generations and cultures. The gap that exists in talent acquisition is that the uniqueness of talent that people with disabilities bring should be recognized and nurtured.

Nearly one in five US adults aged 18 or older (18.3 percent or 44.7 million people) reported a **mental illness** in 2016. In addition, 71 percent of adults reported at least one symptom of stress, such as a headache or feeling overwhelmed or anxious, according to Center for Disease Control. I am pleased to acknowledge the companies that are stepping up to recognize the broader impact of disabilities within their workforce. With the prevalent issue of mental health impacting employees at work, companies had to take notice. Today, it's a business imperative for employees to feel safe to engage company resources to support stress reduction or any other symptoms of mental health.

An example of companies really leveraging disabilities among employees is the path of autism in the workplace, a group with hidden talent. Companies have embraced the unique ability of this group to the extent that jobs are created to leverage their skills in essential functions. I do mean *highly skilled roles* where the abilities of persons on the autistic spectrum align. Yet the reality is that there is a small group of autistic employees.

On the spectrum, we need to be cognitive of the reality of the half million teens and adults that use vocational rehabilitation services for job development but are either under hired or not hired, according to Dr. Shattuck, co-author of the *National Autism Indicators Report*. My question here is, do employers have an obligation to hire this highly functioning labor pool? Or at least seriously consider this group employable? I challenge companies to include this segment in their hiring strategies for more than the uniquely skilled roles; include this segment also for the available opportunities that require essential functions.

We asked companies, *"Do you intentionally recruit persons with disabilities? If so, for how many years?*

✓ **Select one**

Eighty-three percent of companies from the 2019 ILI have intentional strategies in place to recruit persons with disabilities; 48 percent of companies have been recruiting persons with disabilities for more than 10 years.

What is important is for companies to track their activities of engagement to ensure expected results are achieved.

Trends of People with Disability Impact

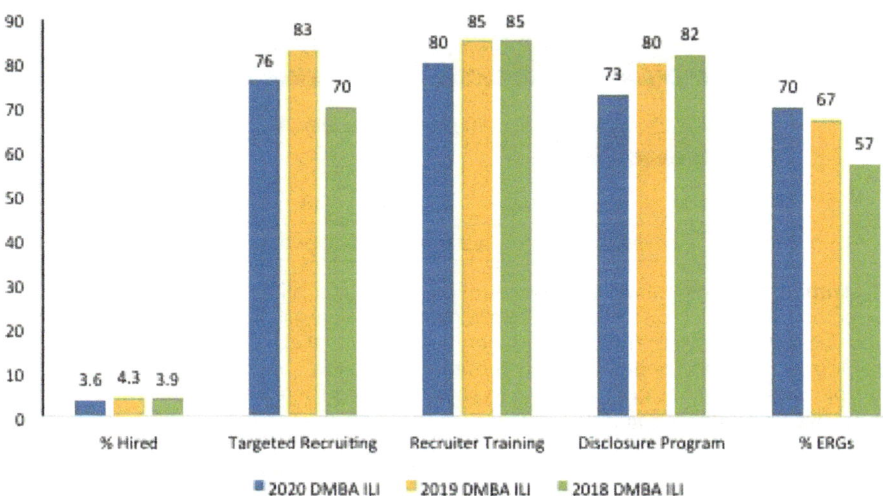

Illustration: The good news is that, over the past two years, I have seen an uptick in the hiring average at 4.3 percent in 2019, up from 2018. The slight decline in 2020 could be from some impact of the pandemic. Unfortunately, it is very low as compared to the national average of annual hiring of persons with disabilities (PWD) at 18.1 percent in 2018, according to Employment Statistics, Department of Labor (DOL). While it is imperative for companies to implement initiatives to drive disability hiring, without metrics and tracking in place, companies are not leveraging their partnerships to achieve better results.

It is forward-thinking for companies to execute strategies for inclusion for persons with disabilities and ensure these employees have a sense of belonging. The efforts for self-identification and full disclosure programs are critical for inclusion to be real. ERGs are not only growing but are a foundational part for organizations to increase opportunities and recruit more persons with disabilities.

We asked companies, *"Have recruiters been trained in unique issues related to hiring persons with disabilities?*

✓ **Check all that apply. The graph below illustrates the results.**

Specific Recruiter Training Trends for PWD

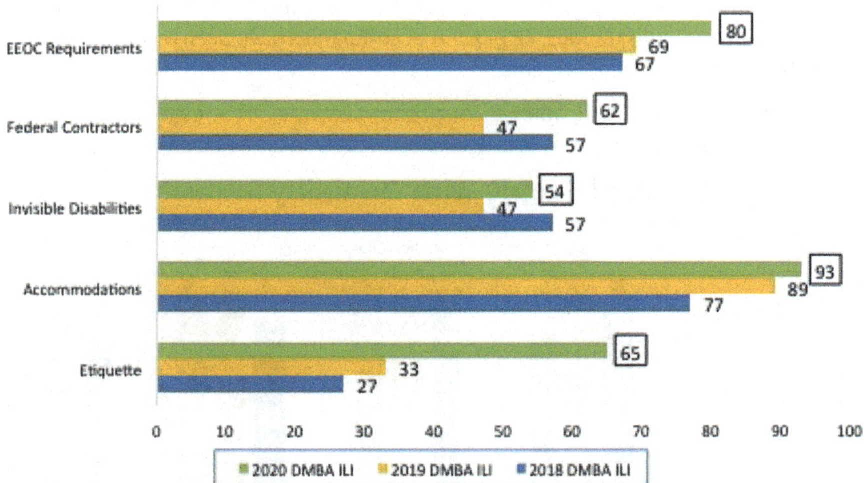

Illustration: This graph illustrates the required training recruiters receive in addition to expected training recruiters require. While diversity training is necessary, it has become a business imperative that recruiters be trained in multifaceted platforms. Etiquette training is a module I began tracking about five years ago. I am discovering that companies are beginning to value having basic training for respect and courtesy as part of the overall required training.

Initiatives to Encourage Full Disclosure

It is equally important for companies to be prepared to encourage full disclosure of employees with disabilities at point of hire. Even though this is an initiative that should be managed internally, I asked companies what special programming is in place to encourage disclosure of disability.

- Adding a place for disclosure on the online application tracking system where this information can be captured for anyone entering the HR system.
- Leveraging employee resource groups to create spaces for people to disclose both visible and/or invisible disabilities.
- Ensuring a reasonable accommodations policy is accessible and available on the company's intranet.
- Hiring an Accessibility Officer who hosts an internal accessibility summit for the purpose of improving accessibility within the company for employees, customers, and job candidates with disabilities.
- Having resources to support employees with family members with disabilities and providing education symposiums for families.
- Engaging senior leaders to share stories regarding their disabilities and to encourage people to self-identify and fully disclose with supporting resources.
- Offering disability awareness sessions on demand to encourage full disclosure.
- Executing an anonymous survey for self-identification several times a year, ensuring employee privacy.
- Conducting a *Break the Silence* campaign – an internal campaign to encourage disclosure through training, awareness, and education.

Best Practices for Hiring People with Disabilities

1. Up your onboarding process: It is a best practice for having persons with disabilities feel better about your company's self-identification process.
2. Enhance your website to attract talent from the disabled population, especially the blind and those with limited audio abilities.
3. Companies need to understand the difference between self-identification and full disclosure so that appropriate and accurate communication is established.
4. Leverage rehab therapists throughout the system to help identify with patients who have overcome barriers and/or obstacles.
5. The best practice is to provide recruiters with more specific training, beyond legal requirements, to broaden their lens and ensure equity in the process.
6. Eighty percent of companies partner with organizations to support disability hiring, yet less than two percent are hired and many companies do not track their efforts. Track your efforts and know who is in your workforce.
7. Best practice sourcing includes tools such as specialized websites so persons with disabilities can find the right opportunities.
8. Establish 90-120-day temp-to-work programs to help persons with disabilities gain workplace exposure and become potential hires.
9. Eighty percent of high school students with disabilities desire to attend college; 60 percent apply to college; and an astounding 40 percent drop out because they do not know where to go for support to get into college or stay in college. Establishing a formal partnership with student groups on college campuses is low-hanging fruit for developing a pipeline for students with disabilities.
10. Create courageous conversations with persons of different abilities to encourage sharing.

Chapter Eight

hire our veterans

"If you are going to achieve excellence in big things, you develop the habit in little matters."
Retired General Colin Powell

I did not want to miss the opportunity to celebrate and recognize the men and women who elect to serve so that we can live in a free world. I often struggle with the disconnect between societal and community perspectives with workplace issues as it relates to veterans. It seems that veterans are all good if they are serving in a military capacity, but once entering the workplace, we seem to think that we must expect something different from a population that is highly skilled.

The good news is employers really get it, thanks to Veteran Jobs Mission. This veterans' initiative began with 11 companies committed to hiring 100,000 veterans. This commitment continues with a coalition of 200-plus companies dedicated to hiring one million veterans. Since 2011, 473,392 veterans have been hired. Learn more by visiting www.veteranjobsmission.com.

If veterans are referred as a great resource for hiring experienced talent, then help me understand... why do we still have this tremendous gap with veterans returning to civilian workforce after service? Unfortunately, the ugly truth is that there are segments of qualified veterans that companies would rather employ. I believe there are underlying biases when it comes to veterans with potential mental illness issues and disabilities. Recruiters have a responsibility to be trained in specific needs for veteran hiring and integration into work culture.

I am not suggesting that companies are only hiring veterans for good citizenship purposes; but they are implementing solid programming. I will share what current and best practices companies are doing to ensure the retention and advancement of veterans.

We asked companies, *"Do you intentionally recruit veterans? And if so, for how many years?*

✓ **Select one**

Ninety-three percent of companies from the 2019 ILI have intentional strategies in place to recruit veterans. Forty-three percent of companies have been recruiting veterans for more than 10 years.

It is critical that companies ensure that the onboarding process is both inclusive and comprehensive.

We asked companies, *"How do you engage veterans in learning?*

✓ **Select all that apply.**

Ninety-two percent of companies use virtual learning as the number one source of communication.

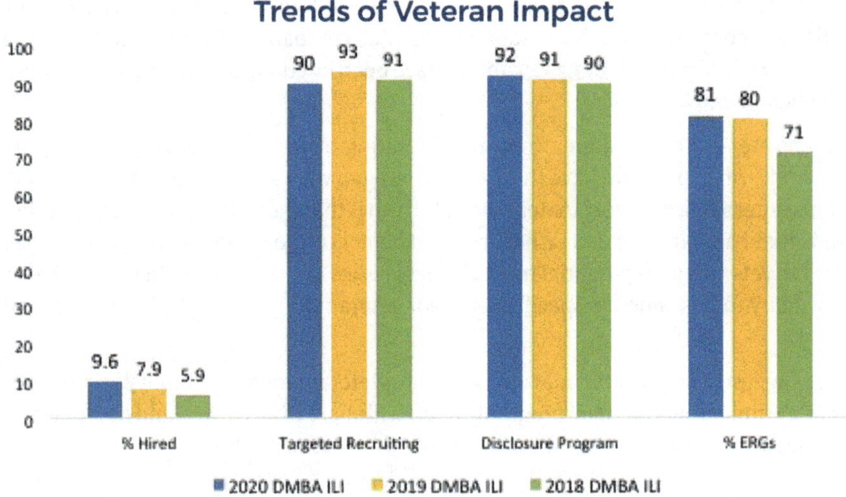

Illustration: 2020 shows the continual advancement of veteran hiring. I do believe that the national hiring initiative for veterans has a tremendous impact on the results. Equally important is that companies recognize that veterans need a supportive culture to function and excel. At the same time, however, companies are struggling with full disclosure with the veteran workforce, like people with disabilities. Veterans with disabilities in the workforce fear disclosure of their invisible disability and/or mental illness. The question is, what can companies do about this very real fear?

Let us not be naïve and ignore the impact of veteran employee resource groups. Their voice is literally what has made the retention of veterans possible. The way companies include employees with military relatives is not just a best practice but a necessary practice. The realities of veteran transition into the workplace comes from the voices of the military resource groups and networks. Year-round initiatives to create inclusion is what I will share in this chapter.

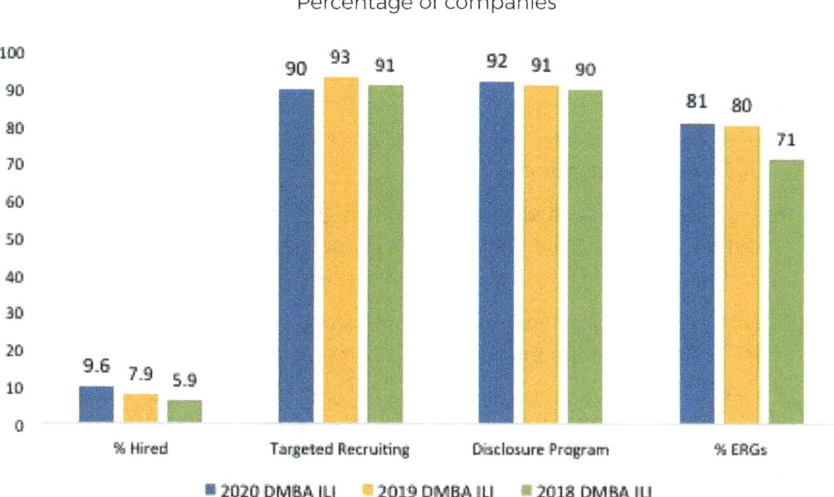

Illustration: This graph illustrates the required training recruiters should receive in addition to the expected diversity training. Disability disclosure initiatives include veterans, yet we still have a gap in training to gain trust from veterans for mental illness indicators. In 2019, Post Traumatic Stress (PTS) training awareness is up with 16 percent of companies implementing this practice. There is not a best practice to date, but companies are trying to determine the best process.

Other veteran training includes specific initiatives companies are exploring to be more inclusive. They range from panel sessions, courses, and training events to creating programs to support military spouses and families. These are the next practices for companies to explore ways to further engage and retain veterans.

Innovative Initiatives to Engage Veterans

Even though companies have committed to hire veterans, I asked companies what special programming is in place to engage veterans in inclusion. Here's a selection of their answers.

- Veteran ERG plans an annual veterans' summit that includes university students as outreach and pipeline development.
- Career and life coaching for veterans and spouses by offering a military support and assistance program.
- Engaging veterans in community partners; such as the Veteran Leadership Program hosted by Wounded Warriors.
- "Have a Beautiful Day" event where veteran men and women bring their spouses to corporate headquarters for a day of beauty, while providing interviewing opportunities.
- Multiple and expanded veteran resource groups that focus on recruitment, self-identification, and full disclosure support creating a culture of belonging and leveraging transferable skills of veterans.
- Establish a virtual military employee resource group and provide programming for leadership, communication, and career growth.
- Linking veterans to the community: Local employer roundtable shares opportunities for veterans to volunteer and connect with their community.
- Establish scholarships for families with veterans and partner with organizations that specifically develop the veteran pipeline.
- Think Tank for Veterans to support strategic company initiatives like recruiting, community, and engagement.
- Partnerships with military bases to learn more about how to transition veterans into civilian workforce.

Best Practices for Hiring and Engaging Veterans

1 Ninety-one percent of companies intentionally recruit veterans; having a dedicated recruiter is a best practice.

2 HR business leaders volunteer to support career placement services for veterans and their families.

3 Forty-eight percent of companies require PTS awareness training for recruiters; expand mental health awareness training as a requirement.

4 Veteran ERGs connect to university military groups and provide mentoring and coaching, establishing a student pipeline.

5 Sixty-four percent of companies have strategic partnerships with veteran-focused organizations for sourcing, engagement, and development.

6 Veteran think tank to stay on top of issues and provide real-time services.

7 Ninety percent of companies have initiatives in place for full disclosure of identification status.

8 Onboarding process that is inclusive of all resources; for example, coaching, mentoring, timetables, etc.

9 Partner with agencies that focus on transitioning veterans from military to civilian life to promote a successful transition to the US workforce.

10 Newly hired veterans have buddies and are paired with mentors to ensure navigation within the workplace.

Chapter Nine

out and equal: *LGBTQ plus pronoun*

"We should indeed keep calm in the face of difference and live our lives in a State of inclusion and wonder at the diversity of humanity."
–George Takei

When I think of tremendous progress, I think of PRIDE recognition: the annual celebration, the gay pride parade, that companies leverage as great support to the LGBTQ Plus Pronoun community, which has achieved national recognition on an annual basis. I do know that, if we go deep within ourselves, we can find ways to celebrate the lives of those who are different year-round. One way to do so is by remembering the purpose of the large parades that occur on a national level recognizing a community that intersects with all ethnicities, genders, veterans, and persons with disabilities. And by the way, they call it the *rise of intersectionality*.

Often, I struggle with the disconnect between societal and community perspectives and workplace issues as they relate to the LGBTQ Plus Pronoun population. The reality is that this is a growing population that contributes significantly to both the workplace and the marketplace. However, there are those who have personal embedded biases, hate, and anger that are devastating in the ways these are acted out, and we appear to be at a loss for action. The Human Rights Campaign index illustrates how organizations are making commitments within their workforce to create parity and equity among the LGBTQ Plus Pronoun workforces. What I mean by this is they capture results in the areas of benefits, full disclosure, and opportunity, etc.

One of the realities in the workplace is that companies have a very challenging job to capture the gay community within their workforce. For one, this group intersects all cultures, generations, and genders. Leveraging employee resource groups helps, but it alone cannot create what is necessary to help this group feel trust in their environment. On average, less than one percent of the LGBTQ Plus Pronoun community in the workforce is identified. Of course, one of the issues is that companies legally cannot request persons to identify sexual orientation or the community they belong to, so that hinders the process.

What do they do? It is the little things that will create great outcomes. Where trust is believed, it will nurture absolution in the workforce. This chapter will focus on intentional strategies companies have implemented to show commitment to hiring this community and engaging them in a culture of inclusion. I hope the insights in this chapter at minimum spark ideas for recruiters and hiring managers to think about so they can improve their results.

The consumer behavior report provided by the Nielsen Diverse Intelligence Series on LGBTQ Plus Pronoun community spending offers insight that helps understanding of the marketing and recruiting value of this group. (For more information: www.nielsendiverseintelligenceserieslgbt).

We asked companies, *"Do you intentionally recruit from the LGBTQ Plus Pronoun organizations? And if so, for how many years?*

✓ **Select one**

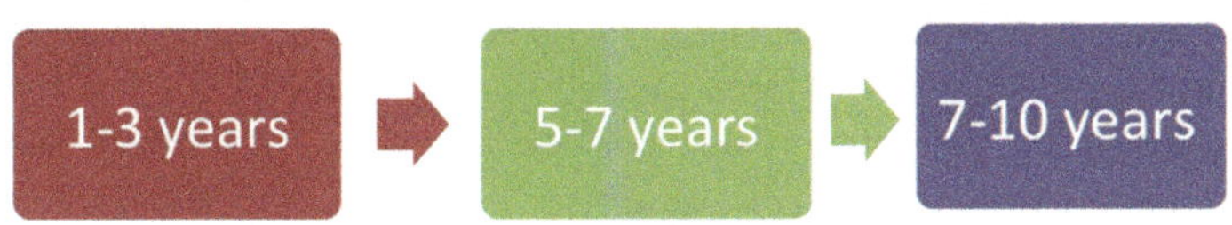

Seventy-three percent of companies from the 2019 ILI have intentional strategies in place to recruit from LGBTQ Plus Pronoun organizations.

Interestingly, on average 13-15 percent of companies have been focused on intentional recruiting in each year grouping. Twenty-three percent of companies are just starting to target this group. Only seven percent of companies have been targeting this group for between seven to 10 years, and it is primarily a new focus for most companies.

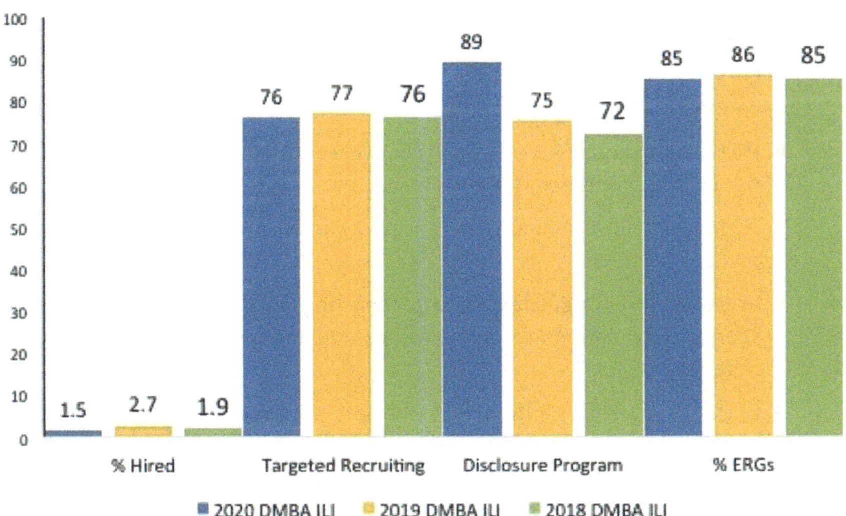

Illustration: Interestingly, I see a correlating increase in the hiring percentages as the pride employee resource groups grow. This correlation also extends to the targeted recruiting efforts and internal efforts of self-identification and disclosure initiatives.

This is the type of analysis and impact we need to see companies making as an integrated approach to how they recruit LGBTQ Plus Pronoun applicants. The indicator is that with the targeted focus of recruitment and the growth of the Pride ERGs, companies must ask the question of *why* identification and upfront disclosure is so difficult. Are there other opportunities to expand training and create safe places for openness still required? And if so, what must you do?

I know that organizations with senior leaders who are out see double-digit results in disclosure. It is simply because the fear factor has been mitigated among those employees. Two percent of a company's workforce has self-identified as LGBTQ Plus Pronoun, as compared to 10 percent of veterans who self-identified and six percent persons with disabilities who have self-identified on average.

Special Programming to Recruit LGBTQ PLUS PRONOUN

While I recognize the efforts companies are taking to partner with organizations to support their LGBTQ Plus Pronoun recruiting efforts, I also wanted to share innovative programming that can attract this group.

- Seventy-six percent of companies have targeted recruiting strategies in 2020, up 10 percent from 2018.
- Dedicate resources to focus on developing strategy, relationships, and local partnerships with organizations for the purpose of recruiting and retention of LGBTQ Plus Pronoun talent.
- Co-sponsorship of community events with LGBTQ Plus Pronoun chamber of commerce to attract seasoned talent.
- Partner with Pride ERG to support college recruiting events and conferences to then interview desired students.
- Partner with local organizations for specific open positions and host education and career forums.
- Pride ERGs are the greatest resource for acting as a think tank for creating new sponsorships, community relationships, and liaisons to diversity councils and other internal teams.
- Leverage advertising with same-sex brands and communications to show the marketplace the company is a great place to work.
- Have a strong presence at national gay and lesbian events for the purpose of recruiting; for example, at the National Gay Medical Association.
- Position employees and managers to participate at conferences as speakers and panelists.
- Ensure that global policies advocating for LGBTQ Plus Pronoun persons in the workplace are protected.
- Create a task force to focus on transgender and gender nonconforming issues to support policy and practices in the workplace.

- Participate in the Human Rights Campaign Index to brand as an inclusive company to work for.
- Participate in the transgender career fair at the LGBTA resource center.
- Hold monthly meetings with the Pride ERG and recruiting team to leverage the existing network for candidates.
- Have dedicated messaging on the company diversity and career sections of the website.

Initiatives to Encourage Full Disclosure & Self Identification of LGBTQ Plus Pronoun Workforce

I asked companies to share what initiatives they have in place to encourage full disclosure among the LGBTQ Plus Pronoun community that lives in their workforce. The initiatives below have had the most impact leading to trust and full disclosure.

- Leveraging employment engagement survey for self-identification and full disclosure. Results have been as high as 60 percent participation year over year.
- Pride ERGs provide the most prolific programming for creating a welcoming and belonging culture. Ensure all programming is expanded to include remote and global employees.
- Fifty-eight percent of companies have expanded their engagement survey to encourage employees to self-identify. It is important that companies consistently update their HR systems to track every employee that self-identifies.
- Sharing stories of LGBTQ Plus Pronoun employees working in the community helped create a celebratory and recognition platform supported by others.
- Partnering with universities where recruiting occurs encouraging participants to fully disclose; the program the Second Look Program.
- Hosting fireside chats with senior leaders to have authentic conversations around the challenges and barriers of self-identification and full disclosure.
- Internal social media campaigns to continually promote full disclosure and self-identification. These campaigns are shared during on-boarding and are optional.

Best Practices for Recruiting and Retaining LGBTQ Plus Pronoun Talent

1. Seventy-five percent of companies have some type of disclosure or self-identification program administered at least once a year.
2. Seventy-seven percent of companies form an affinity or Pride ERG for the purpose of supporting retention.
3. Partner with LGBTQ Plus Pronoun community-focused organizations and LGBTQ Plus Pronoun professional organizations for the purpose of providing local and strategic recruiting activities for this community.
4. Support the national pride parade and include employees and community partners to enhance the company brand and attract exposure.
5. Participate in the Human Rights Campaign Index to benchmark where the company is and what should be done. This also provides branding.
6. Ensure career and diversity sections on the company website illustrate a commitment to LGBTQ Plus Pronoun community and resources.
7. Hold a monthly social media campaign to support awareness and promote self-identification.
8. Establish planning partnerships with Pride ERG with the recruiting team and HR business partners to support hiring managers in achieving goals.
9. Update policies on benefits for partnered households and families.
10. Align global initiatives for LGBTQ Plus Pronoun as close to North American policies as possible.

Chapter Ten

serve up the pipeline: college recruiting

"Recruit me in the places you're afraid to look; you may not see me because I lie in the books."
–Pamela A. McElvane

College or campus recruiting, whichever is your preference, is a process that is embedded with activities and scattered with unsubstantiated outcomes. What I am saying is that not enough companies have a rigid system that helps them identify the best colleges to recruit from. Sadly, employee preferences are added to a large list of colleges that recruiters have collected overtime. This is not a best practice; it is just the practice.

Today, I will admit companies are better focused on planning college recruiting activities. While I am glad to see the progress talent acquisition has made and is making, they seem to be pulling from the same well. This behavior is embedded with processes that are systematic in doing the same thing for the same results. The problem is that there is no real accountability save consequences that impact the outcomes. This chapter is not intended to beat up the college recruiting process but to hopefully provide insights to improve practices.

I remember speaking to a recruiting executive from a large corporation. I asked him, "How many colleges does your company recruit from?"

"About 200 plus; too many to count," answered the executive.

"Wow," I said. "You must have a large team of recruiters to manage such a large college base."

"Well, let's see, I have a team of 15 recruiters," he said.

"Hmm. What is the number of your average open positions per month?" I exclaimed.

"About 10,000."

"Just to be clear, you have 15 recruiters responsible for filling 10,000 positions companywide, monthly, with more than 200 plus colleges to effectively source?"

All I can say is, do the math.

We asked companies, "*Do you recruit from the following institutions?*"

- ✓ **Check all that apply**

Because I am primarily focused on professional occupations, 87 percent of respondents recruit from universities. I am seeing a growing trend of recruiting from community colleges, at 50 percent of companies. Forty-six percent of companies do recruit from a variety of specialty and vocational schools.

The industries that leverage specialty and vocational programs include, but are not limited to, retail, healthcare, manufacturing, and educational institutions.

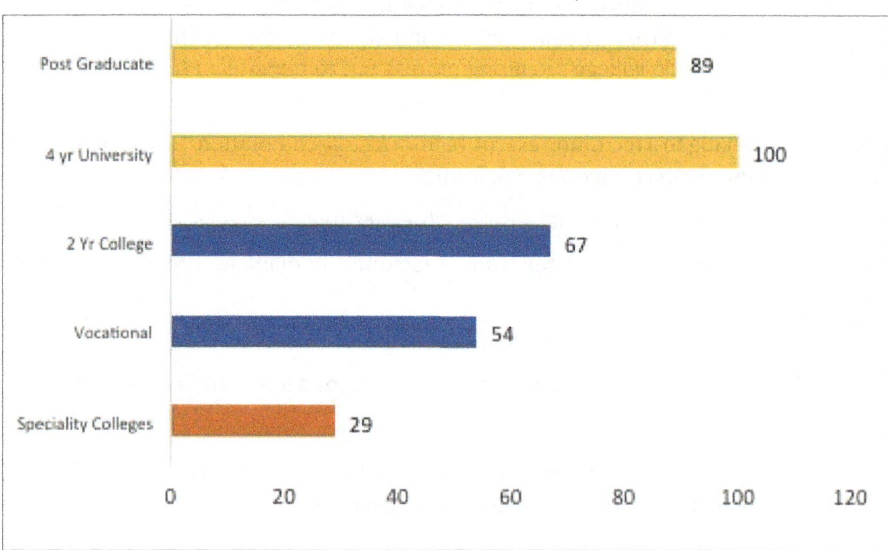

College Recruiting Trends

Intentional Diverse Hiring Results

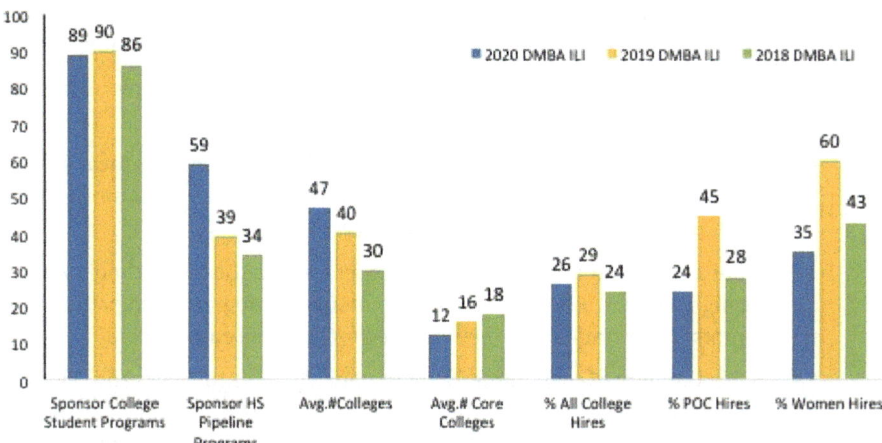

Illustration: Campus recruiting efforts are more focused today as I see the average number of colleges holding at 47. The data shows that 59 percent of companies are identifying specific groups to target on campus and investing in those relationships. There is a direct correlation between special programming and increased hires of women and people of color. Special programming also influences targeting for persons with disabilities, LGBTQ Plus Pronoun, and veteran students.

The sponsoring of campus activities remains high with more than 85 percent of companies engaging in this practice in the past three years. I asked companies to share the most impactful activities that fostered engagement and recruiting pipeline talent. This section is intended to provide insights to validate the good work companies are doing as well as motivate companies to step up their campus activities for engagement.

Campus Activities to Attract Talent & Engagement

- Target HBCU-focused recruiting by hosting resume writing and interview workshops on campus, prepping students for internships. In addition, provide a panel of professionals to discuss career opportunities in the field.
- Through partnership with the Management Leaders of Tomorrow, a company hosted 500 students of color on their campus to introduce them to careers and to executives of color.
- Host planning and career development sessions for student diversity conferences with local partner universities.
- Partner with Jowell, whose purpose is to support the advancement of African American, Latino, and Native American students and professionals. This group provides access to students of color to fill internship opportunities.

- The Global Graduate Program is designed to ensure campus activities for recruitment are aligned with graduate national hiring programs and timelines.
- Leverage community relationships with the YMCA, Urban League, and NAACP to highlight career opportunities and participate in their student career fairs.
- Partner directly with student organizations to host mixers, career sessions, networking events with leaders, etc.
- Recruit a University Relations team for sales positions as they attend classrooms, student clubs, and organizations for women in business. This grassroots direct effort has resulted in successful hires.
- Create a high school-to-work pipeline program with the local school system. The high school students are hired into internship programs and paired with mentors. Upon graduation, they are hired for full-time employment.
- Create a student of color immersion program where 20 colleges send selected students to the company for four days, all expenses paid. Students experience the company culture and how the company showcases its programs and careers.
- Engage the current executive in a college speaking series in colleges where you want to recruit. This gives students an opportunity to hear from your senior leaders.
- Provide scholarships to both high school and college students while they are still completing course work, such as essays and/or case competition participation.
- Sponsor industry and skill-specific programs like Tech Hackathon for women, students of color, and non-binary persons.
- Start a youth apprentice program for local high school students that pipeline to companies for skilled summer employment.
- A summer virtual speaking series was created due to the pandemic and was successful because it was open to all students and allowed for engagement and connection to leaders.
- Create an undergraduate internship program with 100 percent students of color with the focused intention to pipeline students of color.

Campus Recruiting Trends

Formal Internship Program Results

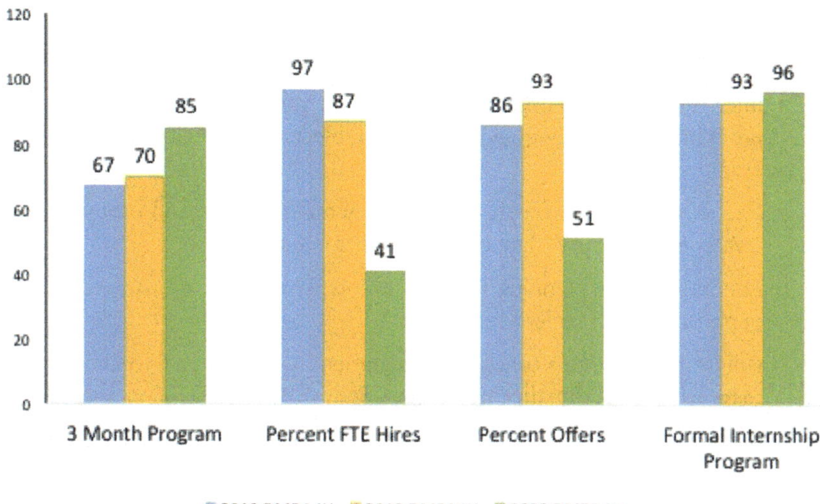

Illustration: Internships continue to be the most effective hiring platform with 93 percent of companies having a formal program and with an average of 87 percent of interns converting to full-time employees (FTEs). The top functional areas for internships are Marketing, Finance, Information Technology, Human Resources, Operations, and Corporate. These functions convert 65 percent of interns to full-time positions on average. Most companies make offers to 75 percent of interns, but the overall acceptance rate is about 30 percent.

Internship Assignments for Career Development

- Interns are assigned to on-the-job projects that align with their course curriculum, so the students receive college credits with the partnering university.
- Create a student pipeline for the cybersecurity program for undergraduates.
- Interns create a Capstone Presentation sharing their real-life experience in the company at the end of their summer session.
- Interns work collectively on a group project and attend weekly professional development sessions.
- Research & Development interns participate in an innovation project to improve current company products with opportunity to develop their own project with final presentation to leadership team.
- Interns are paired with FTEs on a rotational basis to learn real work experience as well as share new thinking with employees; this also includes job shadowing.

- All interns are assigned mentors during their full internship period. Interns also participate in a reverse mentoring program with senior leaders.
- High school students participate in a six-week STEM program partnered with public schools so they can be exposed to project management skills in IT, Marketing, Digital, and Product Development functions.
- Interns serve as volunteers for nonprofits through community give-back programs by providing consulting on projects, partnered with a company employee.
- Interns are partnered with the pharmacy team to learn and conduct opioid awareness training within underserved communities.
- Interns work on planning network events within the company to exercise opportunities for career exploration.
- Full immersion into a consulting assignment with clear goals and objectives, to be achieved within the internship period.
- MBA-level interns work on organizational strategy, market development, and organizational analytics, to name a few. They are key contributors in the function they are assigned.

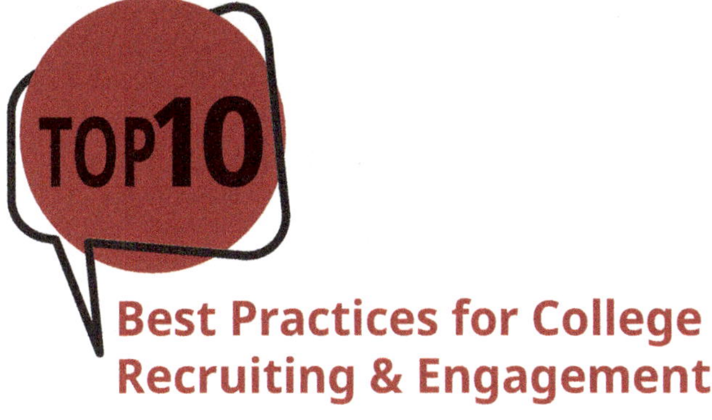

Best Practices for College Recruiting & Engagement

1. Establish a formal internship program with a minimum of a three-month period.
2. Reduce college partnerships to a ratio of five to 10 per recruiter.
3. Engage employee resource groups for targeted recruiting (especially for persons with disabilities, veterans, and LGBTQ Plus Pronoun organizations).
4. Ensure internship program has mentoring component involving leaders.
5. Engage interns in volunteer projects along with their work programs to help them understand value of giving back even while employed.
6. Establish formal planning sessions with talent acquisition, ERGs, and hiring managers to engage college students.
7. Establish a high school pipeline program that is linked to a college internship program.
8. Have dedicated college recruiters with a diversity focus and experience.
9. Engage senior leaders as speakers and panelists at college recruiting events, and host college events on the company campus.
10. Expand recruiting of schools for diverse candidates beyond traditional HBCUs, Hispanic-focused colleges, and include Tier Two and Tier Three programs with diversity programs.

Chapter Eleven

building a diverse applicant pool: filling the gap

"The secret to my success is that we have gone to exceptional lengths to hire the best people in the world."
–Steve Jobs, Former Chairman, CEO & Co-Founder of Apple

They say the secret is in the sauce... I don't think so; it's in the process and the commitment to achieve outstanding results. It is in the effort people are willing to take to ensure they come close to getting what they want. Building talented and diverse applicant pools is a skill; a learned skill, nevertheless. It is built on one failure after the other topped with lesson learned after lesson learned before you get it right for your organization. With that said, you should be able to take a deep breath and breathe. No longer should you think, *am I not doing a good enough job in developing my diverse applicant pool?* If you do not put in the time to get it right, it just will not happen. It is just that simple.

For the purposes of our discussion, let's define *diverse applicant pool* so that we are all on the same page. The applicant pool is the total number of people who have applied for an open position or requisition. Based on the total applicants, the selection process begins to reduce the total applications. In today's environment, diverse has different meanings; it just depends on the lens you are looking through. For our purpose, lets define diverse as representation from the following dimensions of diversity: ethnicity, gender, and identity.

In this chapter, I want to discuss how to leverage diverse applicant pools to build diverse slates and provide options for including diverse talent in the choices you make. There will also be tools to help you think through the process of how to build diverse applicant pools as well as assess existing resources to gauge their effectiveness.

I understand the challenges companies have with leveling the playing field for diverse managers; however, the real problem is that hiring managers and sometimes recruiters give up way too easily, especially if they cannot visualize what success looks like. The reality is that intention, once again, is the ingredient—and there is no secret about it.

DIVERSE APPLICANT POOL DEFINED

Representation

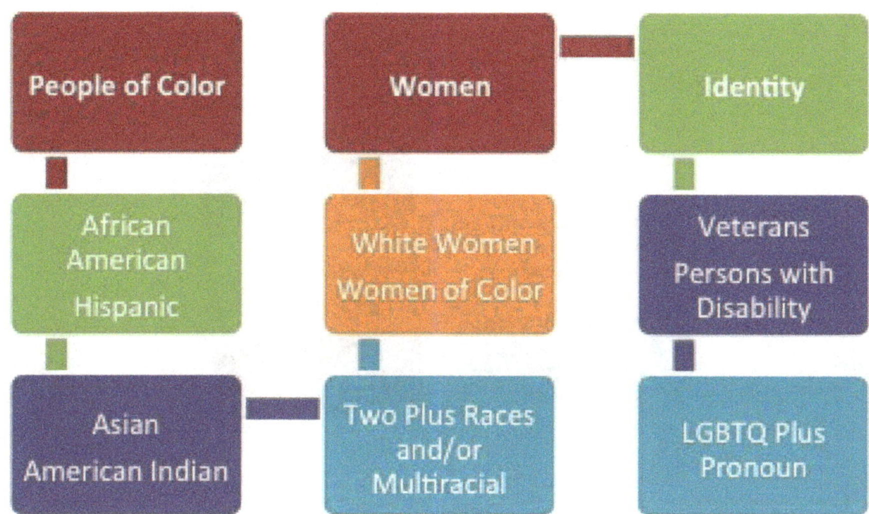

Inclusion

Note: Do not forget about intersectionality. Too often, intersectionality is overlooked and not considered at the time of hiring. It is thought about later, during self-identification and full disclosure programs. *Imagine creating trust on the front-end of interviewing whereby candidates want to share before hired!*

There are a few critical questions each organization must answer: Who is doing the recruiting? Who is doing the hiring? And where are you sourcing? The chart below provides insights on these very items.

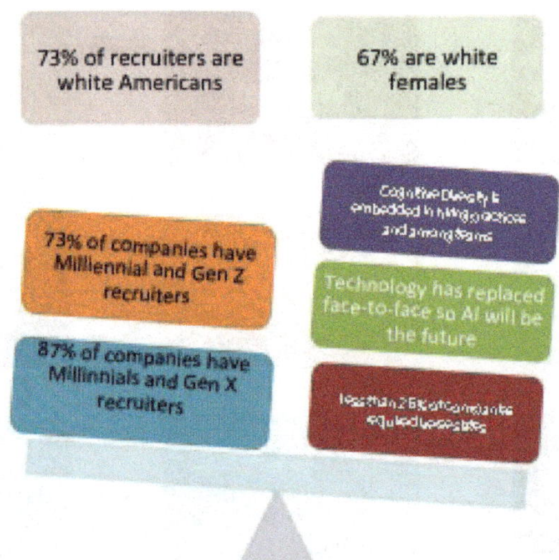

Illustration: Between homogenous recruiters sandwiched with homophobic hiring managers spread with cognitive diversity, this change requires a paradigm shift of how diverse hiring gets done. In a changing world, shifting is the norm. Being agile is part your strategy. And in today's world, technology is the norm in recruiting but leveraging Artificial Intelligence (AI) is the future; just ask Microsoft.

Now that you have defined what diverse applicant pool means to you, let's think through the process of building the applicant pool. Understand that being *intentional*, in this case, is a key component of your process. Moreover, key learnings are important as you think through the effectiveness of your process.

Diverse Applicant Pool Considerations:

- *Hiring teams* should reflect the local population as well as the group you want to recruit. Creativity is key here, using ERGs and other team members.
- *External partnerships* should provide a specific talent pool needed to directly satisfy representation. Professional associations are the number one recruiting source for experienced hires. Relationships with national ethnic and skill-based organizations should be localized.
- *Structure* the type of recruiting team you wish you had by leveraging your hiring managers, ERGs, and leaders. Diversify the group to attract diverse talent.
- *Location* of placement; it is a reality that candidates make choices based on how they will live their lives and connect with the communities in which they work. Headquarter-centric or regionally-based candidates must feel some type of connection to the team they will work with.

- *Population* assessment must be aligned with the ethnic group you are seeking. The reality is that 48 states in North America have a predominate constituency of White Americans. This means if you are going to source talent in a state with a high population density of White Americans, you must be very specific of how and where engagement occurs.
- Recognizing the existence of *subcultures* among every group is the thing that will not change but can be understood and influenced by the intention to provide winning solutions for everyone involved. Equally as important in making the hire is *keeping* the hire. Retention goals are real and early churn impacts the ROI. Retention consideration is a key component of your process; operating without it is a mistake. Just review your results.

We asked companies, *"Do you require diverse slates in recruiting?"*

✓ **Check One:**

Companies that require diverse slates have a formal process in place that is aligned with their diversity recruiting strategy, and have the metrics to measure effectiveness.

We asked companies to share: *"What processes are in place to manage accountability to ensure the effectiveness of diverse slates?'*

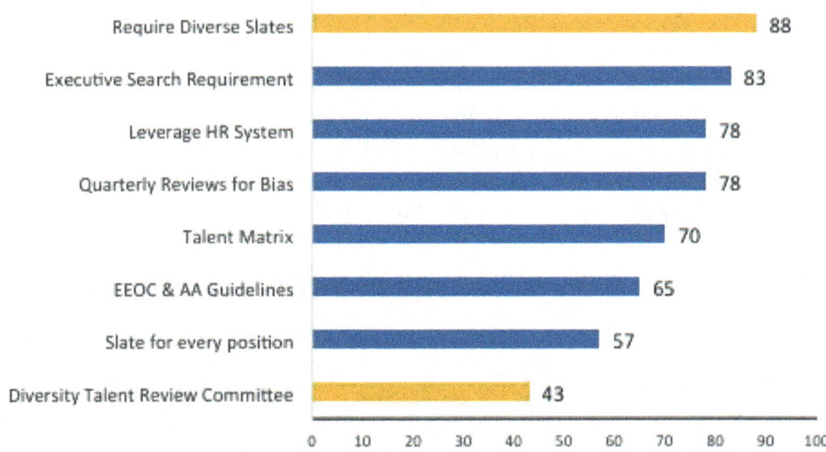

Illustration: Eighty-eight percent of companies require diverse slates, yet less than 30 percent have them aligned to manage accountability and ensure implementation. It is a leading practice to align accountability to the diverse slate process. Leading companies require recruiters to present diverse slates to hiring managers and establish goals for hiring managers that are reviewed in their performance plans.

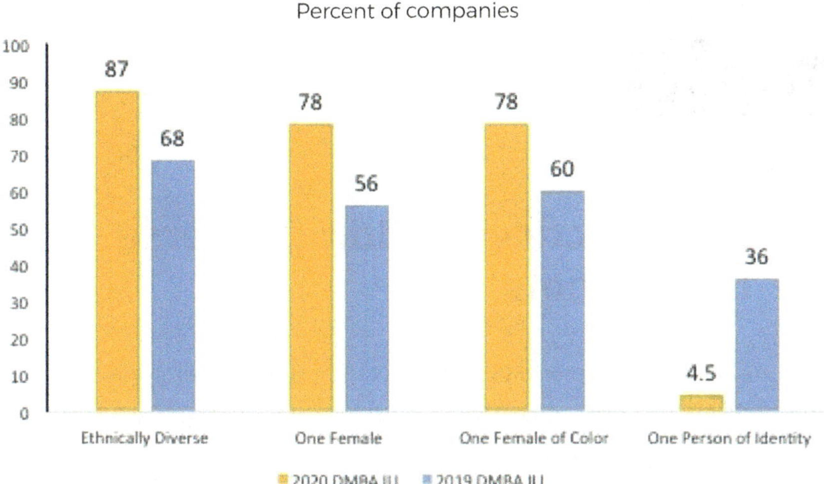

Illustration: As demonstrated by the above chart, 87 percent of companies have ethnically diverse slates to fulfill their requirements. While it is agreeable to have females and self-identifying people (primarily veterans and LGBTQ Plus Pronoun candidates), persons with disability are often not included. However, diverse slates are designed to be the tool recruiters and hiring managers leverage to ensure they are hiring equitably. As seen above, this chart illustrates the potential of reoccurring gaps if the mix is not right and accountability is not certain.

The DMBA ILI has been capturing data on the types of diverse slates companies are leveraging. The good news is that 87 percent of companies understand they must have people of color in every platform. Both White women and women of color have increased, with 78 percent of companies dedicating a position. However, *Harvard Business Review* identified that a slate that has a woman, a woman of color, a diverse person will most likely have a diverse person hired.

Best Practices Building Diverse Talent Pools

1 Dedicated recruiters partner with business units to support identifying and sourcing diverse applicant pools.

2 Eighty percent of companies hire college interns to satisfy diverse hiring goals; ensure your internship program is a part of your diverse recruiting/hiring pool.

3 Build strong college organizational relationships to support campus programming that helps with identifying veterans, persons with disabilities, LGBTQ Plus Pronoun orientation, and people of color.

4 Review existing referral programs and how you engage internal teams to help source talent. Reexamine the effectiveness of internal sourcing.

5 Use crowdsourcing to reach all dimensions of diversity across all generations.

6 Assess existing technologies to ensure you are getting the farthest reach possible for talent unseen (for example; LinkedIn, Facebook, etc.).

7 In today's virtual environment, span the net wide with virtual career fairs, virtual conferences, and many other virtual platforms. Leading companies are leveraging AI to create opportunities.

8 External partnerships should provide a specific talent pool needed to directly satisfy representation. Professional Associations are the number one recruiting source for experienced hires.

9 Require executive search firms and partners to submit a diverse candidate slate that always includes African American and Hispanic males and/or females as this is the largest group companies are seeking to fill management and leadership positions.

10 Recruit simultaneously from the most diverse markets to increase the probability of identifying candidates of color.

CHECKLIST FOR BUILDING & RETAINING A DIVERSE TALENT POOL

- ☐ Consider decentralizing recruiting teams in highly dense areas with diversely populated communities (including the underserved).
- ☐ Train recruiters and hiring managers on diversity hiring practices beyond the required training (for example, mitigating bias in talent acquisition).
- ☐ Enhance talent acquisition recruiting and HR business professionals with diverse persons as the opportunity presents itself.
- ☐ Assess your onboarding to include retention strategies for the first three years. This may mean creating and/or developing buddy programs, early mentoring, and continuous engagement.
- ☐ Ensure talent acquisition has defined what *diverse applicant* means and that all hiring managers are clear on the company definition and goals.
- ☐ Assess the effectiveness of external recruiting partners for sourcing. Also, are they familiar with your goals and aligned with your recruiting team?
- ☐ Be prepared to leverage community and partner relationships to provide candidates with a sense of community upon relocation. For example, offering to pay for a one-year membership to a professional association. Remember, retention works two ways (inside and out).
- ☐ Review Nielsen's diverse intelligence series reports for the most populated markets for people of color at www.diverseinteligenceseries.com and then leverage partnerships and universities in the markets that best suit your needs.

BEST PRACTICES

Implementing the best practices plan

Part IV

Chapter Twelve

establishing metrics to track results

"What gets measured gets managed."
–William Thomson

I suppose, like any other discussion, we must have the accountability conversation just to pulse check how serious you are in making changes. We all know that any type of performance is based on results. And of course, results are defined by... *did I get the return on this investment*? This is true regardless of whether the investment is tangible (cash) or intangible (the time invested to get it done).

I believe in a three-step approach to establishing effective measures to ensure best case results based on current circumstances, changing environmental dynamics, and mandates by any authority you deem accountable. The first step is to determine your goals and the expected time frame for achieving the desired outcome. The second step is to develop KPIs which will allow you to adjust your goals based on circumstances and environmental impacts that prevent you from moving forward. And third, to decide upon the tool you will use to effectively measure progress or the lack thereof. Many organizations use a scorecard, a dashboard, or—the most effective—performance plans. Let's further explore each approach.

I. Goal Setting: Are you kidding me? You think I don't know how to set goals? Of course, you do; this is not my fundamental concern. The reality is that most people establish goals in a vacuum, make decisions, and ask for permission later. It is a business imperative that goal setting for diverse recruiting is a collaborative and inclusive process. The more people at the table with diverse perspectives and experiences the better. This section is simply a reminder of key principles that should be considered in your goal-setting process.

In 1990, Locke and Dr. Gary Latham published *A Theory of Goal Setting and Task Performance* in which they identified five principles that were important in setting goals that will motivate others. Here we are almost three decades later and this process remains relevant. These principles are **clarity**, **challenge**, **commitment**, **feedback**, and **task complexity**.

- **Clarity**

A clear goal is one that can be measured and leaves no room for misunderstanding. Goals should be very explicit regarding which behaviors are pre-desired and will be rewarded. Continue to ask yourself the question, "What will it look like if the goal is completed?" The answer to the question will help you identify clear goals.

Example: Hire five percent African American managers by December 31, 2022; and seven percent Hispanic managers by December 31, 2022.

▪ Challenge

If you know that a goal is a challenge and it is also perceived as such by those who assigned it to you, you are more likely to be motivated to achieve it. Of course, there is a balance to be struck with this principle. A goal should be challenging but must still be achievable.

Example: A challenging goal is to hire African Americans and Hispanics to work in the state of Iowa while only sourcing in the state of Iowa which has a population of less than five percent people of color. Remember not to put yourself in a defined box when managing a challenging goal.

▪ Commitment

For goals to be effective, they need to be agreed upon. The goal should be in line with the general established expectations you have had for the employee in the past. The employee and employer must both be committed to using the resources needed to complete the goal and should also agree on what the reward will be. You could also ask employees to create their own goals for themselves and then discuss them as a team. You might not be aware that someone wants to improve their skills in a certain area or learn more about a specific process.

Example: The commitment from the top is only part of it. You as a recruiter, hiring manager, function leader, executive, or team member must believe this is the best course of action for the organization. If you do not believe that diversity will be a competitive advantage and will enhance the great work your organization is already doing, then, seriously, get another job.

▪ Feedback

What if the person is halfway to completing the goal, but they have a question? What if you suspect that the person is going about the process of completing the goal in the wrong way? Feedback provides a chance to correct or clarify before the goal has been reached.

Example: Establish a monthly or quarterly review process with recruiters, hiring managers, HR Business leaders, diversity council members, and any others who have a stake in achieving the goals. Feedback is the greatest resource you can have.

▪ Task complexity

When a role is complex or highly technical, the person in that role is often already highly motivated or else they would not have reached that level in the organization. However, even the most motivated person can become discouraged if the complexity of the task and the time it takes to complete it was not fully understood. It is important to make sure that the person has enough time to reach the goal. Unreasonable time expectations will drive a person to overwhelm themselves with work and become less effective as their stress level increases.

Example: Include the task leader/manager in the decision-making process on determining the resources needed along the way. Perhaps an additional week is needed to get the specs for the project accurate. Maintain a realism about the work and the requirements for getting it done.

II. Key Performance Indicators: Now that you have established clear goals, it is time to develop KPIs to help you monitor progress. In its simplest form, a KPI is a type of performance measurement that provides you with understanding as to how your organization or department is performing. A good KPI will provide immediate insights whether you are on the right path toward achieving goals.

To be effective, a KPI must:

✓Be well-defined and quantifiable.

✓Be communicated throughout your organization and department.

✓Be crucial to achieving your goal.

✓Be applicable to your Line of Business (LOB), department, or function.

KPIs can be simple or complex. The more easily they are understood by everyone, the better. Depending on your company's structure, develop your own KPIs. Below are 10 KPIs and examples:

1 **Cost:** Measure cost effectiveness and find the best ways to reduce and manage your costs.

2 **Candidates by region:** Through analyzing which regions are meeting sourcing objectives, you can provide better feedback for underperforming regions.

3 **LOB Expenses vs. Budget:** Compare your actual overhead with your forecasted budget. Understanding where you deviated from your plan can help you create a more effective departmental budget in the future.

4 **Number of Applications in Pool:** This performance indicator is straightforward. Identify all your sourcing pools; then, count the number of applications received from each pool. Finally, track the actual number of applications pooled for interviews.

5 **Net Process Score (NPS):** Determining your NPS is one of the best ways to indicate effectiveness of your sourcing and recruiting process. To determine your NPS score, send out quarterly surveys to both recent hires and potential candidates about their experience in the recruiting and interviewing process. Establish a baseline with your first survey and put measures in place that will help those numbers grow quarter to quarter.

6 **LOB Efficiency Measure:** Efficiency can be measured differently in every industry. Use the manufacturing industry as an example. You can measure your organization's efficiency by analyzing how many resumes/interviews you have screened every hour and what percentage of time it took by day, week, etc.

7 **Employee Turnover Rate (ETR):** To determine your ETR, take the number of employees who have departed the company and divide it by the average number of employees. If you have a high ETR, spend some time examining your workplace culture, employment packages, and work environment.

8 **Diverse Slate Submission (DSS):** Based on your company's definition of diverse slate, how many diverse slates were submitted compared to every open requisition/position? What is the number of managers hiring vs. the number of diverse slates submitted for open positions?

9 **Employee Satisfaction**: Happy employees are going to work harder—it's as simple as that. Measuring your employee satisfaction through surveys and other metrics is vital to your departmental and organizational health.

10 **Partnership Sourcing:** Determine the effectiveness of relationships with conferences and partners designed for sourcing and recruiting diverse talent: How much money did it cost to participate vs. how many candidates were identified/interviewed vs. how many candidates were hired.

III. Tools to Measure Progress: The tools we use are as good as the end user. In my humble opinion, it really does not matter how sophisticated the measurement instrument you are using; what matters is that the tools do a few basic things. At minimum, your tools should measure progress, identify gaps, and provide action steps to support behavior changes.

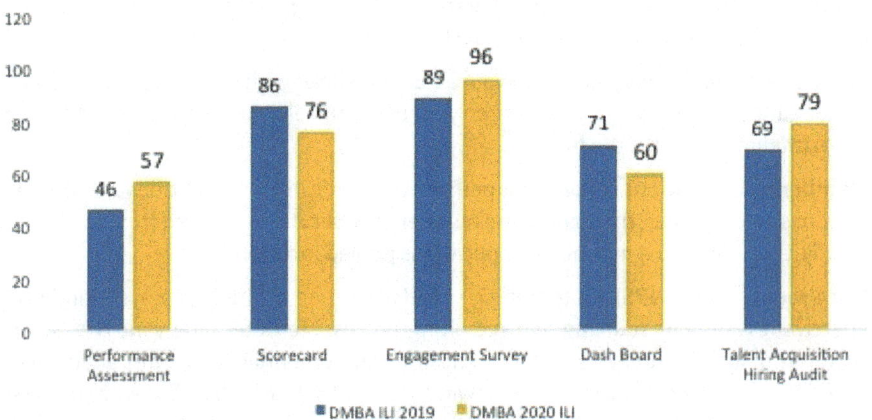

Illustration: The most popular tools among companies are score cards, engagement surveys, and dashboards. However, the tools that allow for a deeper dive are employee performance assessments, retention insights, and talent acquisition hiring audits.

The best practice is to use three to five different tools to support insights and accuracy for the integration of new strategies that will drive change. Seventy percent of companies leverage more than two tools to support effective measures.

When built successfully, the use of Scorecards can facilitate communication between different departments in an organization, help create alignment, and help groups make smarter budgeting decisions.

Illustration: Miriam Webster

HOW TO BUILD A SCORECARD

Many organizations hire experts to help build score cards and dashboards, but you can build your own. Below is an example scorecard. You can name it for your function once you identify goals with departmental alignment.

	A	B	C	D	E	F
1	**Vision**	World Class Leadership				
2		**Objectives**	**Measures**	**Targets**	**Initiatives**	**Results**
3	**Satisfy Shareholders**	Increase Customers	Number of Customers	% increase		
4		Increase Order Size	Average Sale	% increase		
5		Increase Frequency	Frequency of Sale	% increase		
6		Increase New Product Revenu	# New Products % New Revenue	% increase		
7						
8	**Delight Customers**	Increase Customer Satisfactio	Customer Satisfactio	% increase		
9		Reduce Customer Complaints	Complaints	% reduction		
10		Increase Referals	Number of Referrals	% increase		
11		Increase Frequency	Frequency of Sale	% increase		
12						
13	**Effective Processes**	Reduce Cycle or Lead Time	Cycle Time	% reduction		
14		Reduce Defects	DPMO	% reduction		
15		Reduce Costs	Cost of waste & rewo	% reduction		
16						
17	**Motivated & Prepared**	Increase Core Skills	Training	% increase		
18	**Workforce**	Reduce Employee Turnover	Turnover	% reduction		
19		Increase Systems Availability	Unavailability	% reduction		

Eight steps to building your score card:

1. Assessment—complete function assessment to identify gaps and opportunities.
2. Strategy—ensure talent acquisition and diversity strategies are aligned with target recruiting.
3. Objectives—ensure goals are aligned with strategic business objectives.
4. Strategy Map—this is always good to have as a snapshot of goals and objectives.
5. Performance Objectives—should be outlined in individual contributor's goals.
6. Initiatives—should be measurable and quantifiable.
7. Performance Analysis—should allow you to identify successes and gaps so change can occur quickly.
8. Alignment—needs to be inclusive of everyone not just in writing but in philosophy and commitment

EXERCISE: Build your Score Card for Diversity Recruiting

Diversity Recruiting

	Objectives	Measures	Targets	Initiatives	Results
Financial					
Customer					
Effective Process					
Train & Develop Recruiting/Hiring Managers					

Chapter Thirteen

build your own: recruiting best practice case study

"My own career is a case study for what I believe in."
–Simon Sinek

Case studies, if not done properly, can be misused in creating a compelling story to help solve challenging problems. Case studies can be very effective in creating engagement with your team when solving a problem. My approach here is to provide a case study as a learning platform that can be easily duplicated for other business initiatives that need more attention. According to David Chapman, CEO of Forma, there are eight principles to building an effective case study. The reason I want to share this with you is because I believe you should know how to build your own effective case studies to create a continuum of learning.

Before I dive into our case study of the Best-in-Class Diversity Recruiting Framework, let's review the eight principles of developing a case study.

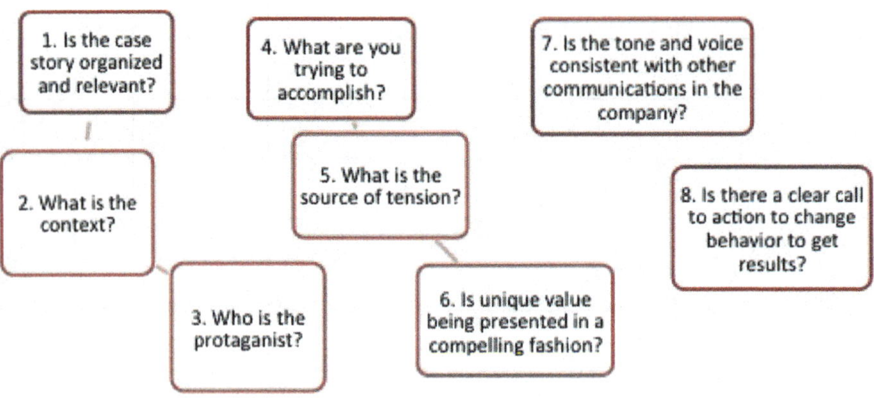

ROAD MAP TO DEVELOPING A BEST PRACTICES CASE STUDY

To the best of your ability, I need you to answer truthfully the following questions to develop the case study problem that will allow for change in your talent acquisition process to hire diverse talent.

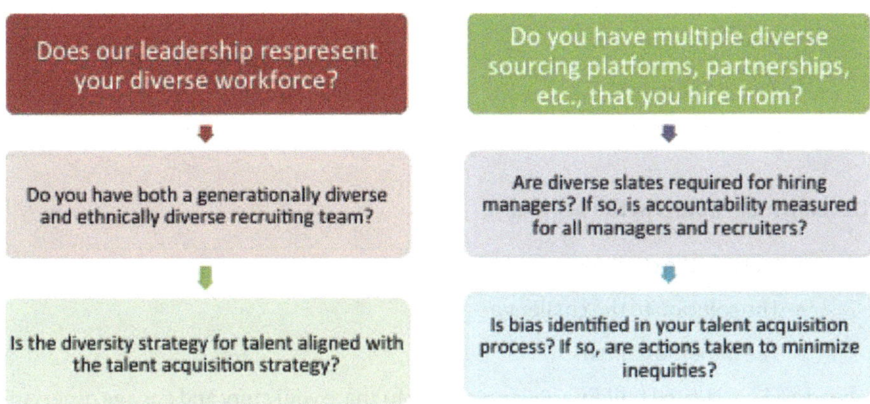

Identify the activities and current initiatives you have in place to lay out your roadmap of what you have achieved.

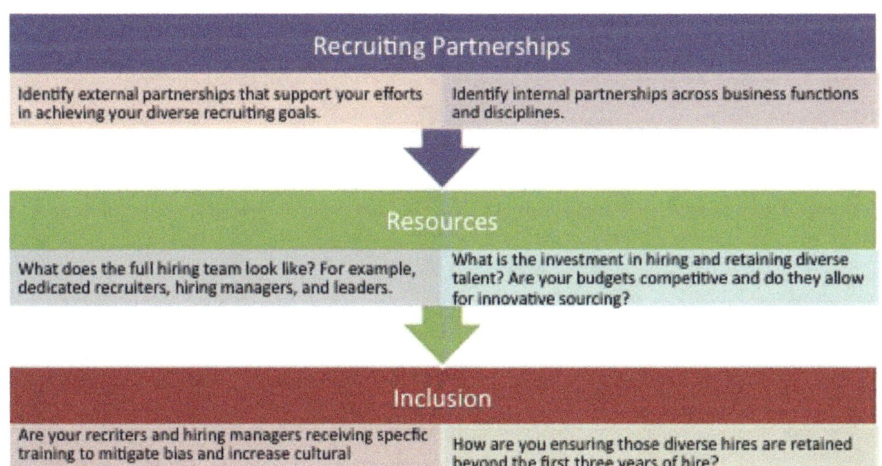

Key Elements of a Case Study

1. **Start with the five W's**
   - Who's Involved,
   - What Happened,
   - Where's it happening,
   - When it occurs and
   - Why it is happening

2. **Develop main points in the beginning**
   - Identify the challenge
   - The solution to the challenge
   - The benefits gained

Go ahead and get started building your case study to share your story and engage others to help you achieve the changes that you desire.

Prologue

Is diverse talent really this hard to find? Or are you looking in the wrong places, or worse, not looking at all?

My grandmother Odessa Coleman is over 100 years old. I suspect rather cynically that the question of where and how to find diverse talent has not changed much over those 100 years. A quick reflection would indicate that the collective pool of diverse talent has certainly grown and become more available through the years.

However, leadership and courage are necessary to incubate an environment that allows management and recruiters to promote and sustain diversity talent sourcing. I started my early career as college relations staffer and an internal staffer. From the beginning of my career until the end, the key question never changed...how can I find and identify diverse talent? The irony of this was that I always believed that I was surrounded by diverse talent. Corporation after corporation seemed to be faced with this seminal question!

Again, I respond it is not what you are looking for only. The where and how you are looking for talent is key and critical.

The team must be guided by a common set of principles such as: 1) increasing shareholder value, 2) alignment with your customer base, and 3) shared corporate/employee values.

Most organizations set out to do the right thing, but somehow get derailed along their route to success. As we learned in economic class where supply equals demand there is a perfect union. If it is true that demand far outstrips supply, then innovation and focus should be turned up to correct this imbalance. Yes, my grandmother would say over her 100 plus years, the diverse pool of talent has significantly improved but many would argue in the context of today's question that not enough talent has found their way to the many corporate and board opportunities available today. Progress but not success... Why is that?

Pam McElvane has set out in her descriptive "how to book" to align the question with a programmatic solution. Ms. McElvane lays out a methodical playbook as to how you assess your strategy, and then address your diverse talent recruitment plan. She has been on the frontline of this issue through her Diversity MBA efforts by gaining insights of progressive steps that go beyond simply checking the box or creating the obligatory must do activities. She knows and shares with you that by connecting the right diverse talent to your organization, significant shareholder value can be created. Who owns this plan is critical to its success. Pushing it down the line to HR (Human Resources) is another way of avoiding a critical obligation of the management team and the board. There should be top- down involvement through the life cycle of this recruitment plan.

But of course, getting diverse talent is phase one, retaining the talent is phase two. The plans must be coherent and aligned. I am looking forward to the next installation of the SKINY series to lead us to a workable framework for the next phase.

Michael Millegan, Independent Board Director, and Retired Global President, Verizon Communications

APPENDIX

CONTRIBUTING THOUGHT LEADERS

This section is intended to allow thought leaders in the diversity, equity, and inclusion space to provide perspectives that will support developing strategies for diversity recruiting and retention. These leaders write about strategy, metrics, recruiting, management and more. The point is that you, the reader, can contribute to this process by leveraging your experiences.

I extend a heartfelt thank you to the leaders that took the time out of their busy schedules to share their expertise and for supporting me in my first book.

Strategy

What is a Strategy?
Fundamentals of Successful Strategic Planning

Have you ever noticed how the question of "What is a strategy?" rarely comes up in the context of strategic planning? The word strategy is frequently used with the assumption that anyone involved in developing strategies knows exactly what a strategy is. It has been my experience that such an assumption is often wrong. Far too often, those charged with the task of strategic planning for their organization do not know or understand the definition of strategy. The result is that what they end up calling a strategy is not really a strategy. With this consequence in mind, I'll start by discussing what a strategy is not.

Before I begin, please keep in mind that the goal of this discussion is not to get caught up in semantics. The goal is for you and your planning team to have a unified basis for evaluating ideas so that you can begin the process of deliberately converting ideas into actionable strategies.

Strategy versus Tactic

As a strategic planning expert for more than 15 years, it has been the case most often that I am given a series of tactics when I ask a potential client what their current strategy is for achieving their objective. Most people think they have a strategy when all they really have are tactics. This confusion is common and can undermine the entire strategic planning process. It will serve your strategic planning efforts well to understand and be able to distinguish strategies versus tactics.

Tactics are specific actions that promote achievement of a strategy. The hierarchical order goes like this:

A tactic supports achievement of a strategy.
A strategy supports achievement of an objective.
An objective supports achievement of a mission.
A mission supports achievement of a vision.
Achievement of a vision fulfills purpose.

Only having tactics without actionable and integrated strategies is a primary reason why so many business owners and executives are frustrated and simply spinning their wheels. In other words, they are busier than ever before and investing significant resources, but not experiencing significant progress on their objectives or anything close to the expected return on their investment. Please do not think for a moment that tactics play a less valuable role in the success of an objective. The right tactics are just as important as the right strategy.

What is a Strategy?

In its simplest form, a strategy is a clear decision and statement about a chosen course of action for obtaining a specific goal or result. While this definition is succinct and suffices for a general discussion, this definition and those like it have no practical value for organizational strategic planning efforts. Why? It provides no basis for evaluating whether a strategy is actionable. Actionable strategies are the only kind that matter in business.

What is an Actionable Strategy?

From the perspective of successful strategic planning, there are two kinds of strategies: actionable strategies and all other strategies. My definition of an actionable strategy states:

An actionable strategy is a comprehensively scrutinized decision about the most effective and efficient use of specific resources for systematically increasing competitive advantage and profits over a specific period of time.

Sidenote: If increasing competitive advantage and profits over a specific period of time is not the goal of your current strategic planning efforts, then just substitute your goal in this definition to make it specific to your needs.

Actionable strategies are a fundamental part of the Actionable Strategic Planning® process as they support business growth in multiple ways and enhance your chances of success if the right minds are engaged in consistently monitoring, evaluating and integrating new information and adapting the strategy as necessary.

Sherrin Ingram, Author, CEO Ingram & Associates replace with Sherrin Ingram, J.D. CEO Ingram & Associates, and Best-Selling Author, 13 Books.

Recruitment through the Lens of Business Strategy

In today's world of business, a company's poorly designed diversity recruitment strategy that lacks cultural understanding about varied candidates will result in losing top diverse applicants to its competitors. Talented employees are critical to sustainable business growth and success. Nonetheless, if a company seeks to hire top diverse talent, they must first attract and recruit them in ways that are efficient and effective. If a company's recruitment effort is not properly thought through, the results will yield negative hiring outcomes and lost productivity, which will result in lost revenue (Breaugh, 2009).

The business case for addressing the gaps within workforce diversity has heightened due to changing employee trends and population indicators, which show that cultural diversity in the workplace has directly impacted business success in the past and will likely do the same in the future. Changing demographics in the United States continue to impact the ways in which companies attract, hire and retain top diverse talent. In the last 10 years, the population within the United States has shifted rapidly due to increasing groups of non-white citizens living in various regions across the country. However, this continuing shift has not reflected much change in workforce hiring and leadership representation in many companies (Robinson, Pfeffer & Buccigrossi, 2003).

Many companies have tried to address these workforce disparities by hiring diverse individuals in high volume. Even so, this type of quick fix strategic approach has not yielded success in sustainability and scalability across any industry. In order to alleviate this lack of duration, some companies have developed an updated holistic diversity and inclusion approach to address the root of the problem that is built around the cultural competence acumen and identifying the unconscious biases of hiring managers and leaders (Egan, 2013).

In the past, diversity training programs and initiatives commonly focused on affirmative action, equal employment opportunity and compliance training. Organizations have recently uncovered how to connect business development opportunities and diverse workforce engagement as an integrated strategic imperative to increase diverse market share and build employer brands within their industry. As a result, some top Fortune 500 companies accelerated their diversity and inclusion journeys to concentrate on unconscious bias in order to increase the knowledge of individual bias, cultural differences and other dimensions of diversity that are relevant to this process. For example, some unconscious bias learning includes the need to address the overarching challenges and struggles that companies face when dealing with personal stereotype and discriminatory behavior from managers (Lubin, 2014).

Five years ago, companies offered and implemented diversity learning programs; but only 2% of those organizations provided content on unconscious bias. However, the projection for the next five years is that 50% of companies will offer some type of unconscious bias learning in order to address the struggles and challenges in attracting and hiring top diverse talent (Lubin, 2014). Margret Reagan – the head of FutureWorks Institute and a known global diversity and inclusion consultant – predicts that companies will need to address the intelligence gap within unconscious bias so that they can clearly communicate the important decisions hiring managers make when companies consistently make efforts to attract the best diverse talent (Lubin, 2014).

Hiring and retaining top diverse talent has been a consistent challenge within many companies, and – historically – federal programs have not yielded the adequate results needed to increase workforce diversity, even though explicit initiatives like the affirmative action have been put in place for the very purpose of increasing diverse workforce representation. Certain characteristics (like the lack of cultural diversity awareness in the workplace, unchanged recruitment processes, and the impact of unconscious bias) have prevailed through these efforts, stymieing the progress in advancing diversity representation within companies (Lubin, 2014). In order to succeed in today's world, organizations must seek to appreciate the effect of cultural diversity in the workplace, to review the common recruitment process and to understand the impact of unconscious bias in hiring practices.

Andrew Lee, PhD, Chief Diversity Officer, Seattle Children's Hospital

Metrics

Diversity, Equity & Inclusion (DEI) Metrics

There are many ways to measure the impact of how companies are advancing DEI. Some companies spend thousands of dollars hiring consultants to do it for them, yet some pull together endless of reams of pages with all sorts of data points. After 28+ years in the DEI space, I have learned it is best to keep things simple, especially if you want your business leaders to understand and support your efforts.

Keeping Things Simple:

The critical metrics you should really be looking at: Acquisition data, Performance Ratings, Promotions, and Turnover.

- **Acquisition**: You will want to look at the data of who is being hired by the various business functions. Specifically you will want to look at the number of applicants being considered, the percentage being hired by race/ethnicity, gender, disability and veteran status. It is important to set hiring goals at a national, local and global level and then track hiring against those goals. As a D&I practitioner you will want to partner with the head of Talent Acquisition and the Human Resources (HR).
- **Performance Ratings**: You will want your HR and Talent Management team to review the performance ratings of management employees by race, gender, etc. by function to see if there are any patterns of any particular group receiving lower ratings. This measurement allows the business and HR to determine if a particular group is being impacted disproportionately. For instance, four women on a team of 10 end up with the lowest rating of anyone on the team. This is usually an indicator that HR should look at a pattern of behavior that maybe impacting the women from advancing or being rewarded at the same rate as the men in the group.
- **Promotions**: Taking a deep dive into succession plans and promotions is critical from a business perspective. If a company is spending money to hire ethnically diverse and female, etc. and they are not advancing at the same rate as the majority population within the company, then you may end up with a leaky talent bucket. It is critical to work with Talent Management to understand who is being advanced and who is being placed on succession plans. Analyzing the data can help you determine where to focus your energy in the organization to help it eliminate any intentional or unintentional bias in the advancement of talent.
- **Turnover:** If your company has a leaky bucket because talent is leaving every 12-24 months, then your company's culture may be impacting your ability to effectively retain talent. By partnering with HR to track and review turnover rates by line of business, ethnicity, gender, etc. you will be able to spot patterns within business functions where there may be a diversity issue. A lot of business leaders do not understand that there is a hidden cost to turnover, the cost for each departure is equivalent to a year's salary + the cost of hiring + the investment in learning.

Dashboards, Scorecards, Trackers...Oh My

Regardless of the format you use, keep it simple. I try to just have one page that HR and Business Leaders can speak too. The more complicated the format, the less likely you will get buy-in/support. At one particular company, the head of diversity had an analytics team in place that created a 10-15 page report for each manager looking at metrics. The reports were barely or never used. At another company they had a three- page report but managers also didn't use it.

At the end of the day, a one-pager works best. Additionally, you will want to make sure that the items you focus on tracking are part of the manager, business leaders', VPs' or Presidents' and CEO's business scorecard. When DEI metrics are part of the business operations scorecard, you will get more traction.

Partnering with Human Resources & Your Line of Business Managers and Leaders

The Line of Business Managers and Leaders are critical partners to helping champion cultural change. While you may provide training, coaching, and/or track talent metrics, business leaders need to have a financial reason as to why supporting DEI so changing their behavior is critical.

Human Resources, Talent Management and Talent Acquisition are critical partners in helping you to analyze and identify patterns that may negatively impact the company. These three groups are very important business in driving organizational change and understanding. Obtaining input on the development of a one-pager that can be used by your HR Business Partners (HRBPs) and the business leaders that are part of your company can help you significantly advance the conversations on DEI.

The HRBPs often lead business discussions on and during the talent review process, and the questions they ask can help influence business leaders' decisions about who is being considered for promotions, special assignments or leadership development opportunities. They can also be on the lookout for unconscious bias or comments that may pop up during these discussions. For instance a manager that makes a comment about, "I am not sure that Casie is ready for a new assignment because she just had a baby." On the surface this may seem like an innocent comment of concern, but the reality is that this type of comment calls into question whether Casie is capable of performing in a leadership capacity. While that might not be the intent, the comment is not relevant to job performance. Additionally, if Casie was a male, having a new baby at home would not be brought up as a reason for not providing a news assignment. An HRBP can help steer the conversation through questions back to a place where potentially undermining comments can be set aside.

Resources to Define Workforce Goals

Bureau of Labor Statistics: www.bls.gov is a great resource of workforce representation by industry.

Specific Industry Associations: National Marketing Association, National Association of Manufacturing, American Institute of Certified Professionals in Accounting. These association collect market data on talent availability in their professions and are a great resource on benchmarks for what the best in class companies are doing to close diversity talent gaps.

In the end keep things simple. Don't waste money on major consultants who will charge you $25K or more dollars to pull information together that your HR partners and internal data analysts can help you pull together. Start simple and get buy-in from your business leaders on the metrics that can be incorporated into their existing business scorecards. Apply the dollars saved to programs and initiatives designed to develop and retain talent.

Nereida (Neddy) Perez, Global Chief Diversity Officer at McCormick & Company.

Driving Business Results Through Selection, Retention and Inclusion

People are the driving force of organizations, and thus the selection and retention of the right people can make or break an organization. To find the right people, we must accurately assess their skills, experience and ability to create broad networks. How can we do this?

Focus on people outcomes that drive business results.

We must determine what business outcome we want to achieve and determine what talent we need to achieve it. This makes the selection and retention of diverse talent even more important to drive strong business results.

As leaders request new roles for their organization, clear outcomes for the roles must be defined, and appropriate behavioral questions designed in order to assess abilities and select the right people. This approach may be challenging, as many HR professionals focus on supporting the leader instead of challenging the leaders' thinking about selection. However, with this approach, the HR professional can avoid the pit of selection for the elusive "fit" and can recruit for business outcomes rather than support the leader's agenda, resulting in a balanced and bias-free selection process.

The same approach should be applied to development and retention. Succession management processes should be clearly established and allow HR professionals to push back when leaders' employee selections are not supported by objective data.

This approach is risky, as not all HR leaders believe they have their organizations' support to push back against leaders' biased approaches. The approach requires HR to be nontraditional and transformational. The data shared must be focused on how the employee's performance drives business results. If growth is a company goal, this approach to talent could change the organization's growth trajectory of your company.

How inclusive are your teams and new hires?

Is your organization ready for diverse talent? An organization must be prepared to embrace and fully leverage incoming talent so that the new employee is appropriately valued and the maximum productivity is realized from the hire.

We should always ask what diverse skills an employee brings to the table and whether they can deliver the necessary performance to drive results. Asking about their networks evaluates their openness to be more inclusive.

Diverse networks drive creative results.

Broad networks are an indication of inclusivity. Hiring inclusive people will progressively make your organization more diverse and inclusive, as they will bring more people like themselves to your organization. I recently networked with an Asian male CEO who was concerned that, despite his business's success, he had not been successful in attracting a diverse team. The reason for this was that his network was not sufficiently diverse; by diversifying his network, he could increase his team's diversity and thus grow his results.

Human Resource leaders must build the diversity blueprint for leaders to follow. Ensure that your networks are diverse enough to hire the right people to execute the organization's business plans, ultimately driving organizational profit.

Anise Wiley-Little is the author of ***Profitable Diversity: How Economic Inclusion Can Lead to Success****, former Chief Human Capital and Diversity Officer for the Kellogg School of Management at Northwestern University and retired Vice President of Human Resources and Chief Diversity Officer for Allstate Insurance Company.*

Actionable Steps

Building a Diverse Workforce through Intention & Inclusion

The business world, especially retail landscape, is evolving rapidly, and if we want to thrive in the new era, we must be innovative and agile like a start-up to meet the changing wants and needs of our customers. We have been committed to building a diverse workforce and fostering an inclusive culture where every one of our 2.4 million associates around the world is valued and empowered to fulfill their full potential and well-equipped to better serve our customers. To achieve that commitment, we must integrate culture, diversity and inclusion into every facet of the associate career life cycle from recruitment, hiring, development and promotion to retirement.

We believe that building a diverse workforce requires deliberate and purposeful choices beginning with the talent supply chain. Having a systemic strategy and structured processes are critical to tackling the current challenges such as limited talent pool, tightened labor market, scarcity of new skills and turnover.

- Branding and Positioning - Showcase diversity and inclusion (D&I) is genuinely woven into the company and talent life cycle
    - Integrate D&I message into the Career portal and corporate websites;
    - Leverage social media to tell D&I success stories and program efforts; and
    - Build a brand image as a D&I leader to attract diverse talent.
- Job Posting - Position the company as an inclusive employer
    - Job posting plays an important role in recruiting talent and often provides the first impression of a company's culture. Avoid masculine words like competitive, confident, outspoken and use words like cooperative, honest, loyal and understanding in job postings; and
    - Choose keywords to maximize diversity sourcing efforts. Build them into our recruiter search strings to focus on applicants we want to recruit.
- Diverse Slates - Require Diverse Slate for open positions
    - Require recruiters to provide at least one diverse interview slate for every open requisition for senior management positions;
    - Recommend a diverse interview panel for selection decisions; and
    - Develop a scorecard to track and report the progress of Diverse Slate practice.
- Diverse Talent Source - Expand the efforts to build relationships with diverse talent sources
    - Partner with schools with a large minority base to establish a solid source of recruiting. The National Association of Colleges and Employers provides diversity resources to companies, including a list of minority institutions and diversity statistics for minority schools;

  - Leverage professional associations that cater to diverse candidates, including networking groups, alumni associations and other networks that already function as a hub;
  - Seek out influential community-based organizations to nurture meaningful and mutually beneficial relationships; and
  - Support selected diversity career fairs to bring in top diverse talent.
- Unconscious Bias - Mitigate unconscious bias during recruiting and hiring processes
  - Require recruiters and hiring managers to participate in the Unconscious Bias training to raise awareness and learn how to minimize implicit bias in the recruiting and hiring processes
  - Change certain recruiting and interviewing methods to be more anonymous, diminishing potential bias and providing the candidate the opportunity to prove they know how to do the work we are asking of them; and
  - Use Inclusion Education to teach managers how to embrace diversity through inclusive leadership and team dynamics.
- Accountability - Track and measure the success of diversity recruiting and hiring
  - Identify key measures to sustain the success of diversity recruiting and hiring; and
  - Develop a scorecard to regularly report the progress.

The diversity recruiting and hiring is just the starting point of the overall diversity and inclusion efforts. Fostering an inclusive environment plays an even greater role in engaging and retaining a diverse workforce. It takes another space to explore this topic.

By Donald Fan, Senior Director, Culture, Diversity & Inclusion, Walmart, Inc.

Three Best Practices in Diverse Recruiting

DIVERSE SLATES

Do you want to increase the odds of a diverse hire by 200 times? Use the two-key rule instead of the Rooney Rule.

We all know the Practice called the Rooney Rule, derived from football, that refers to having at least one diverse candidate on the slate. The thinking behind the rule is to increase the odds of a diverse candidate being selected.

The reality is that evidence does not point to the above outcome as often as we might assume. Depending on how many steps exist after the slate formulation, with the total candidates, the odds of the diverse candidate being selected does not improve consistently.

There is a Best Practice that improves the odds of a diverse candidate being selected by 200 times, with the selection of a female candidate by 80 times.

Controlled experiments done by the University of Colorado indicate that if there are two diverse female candidates on the finalist list, the odds of the selection of one of them increase dramatically, in the above range, regardless of the total number of finalists.

SCORECARDS WITH MULTIPLIERS

Want to increase senior executive commitment to enhancing diversity at your company by 30 times? Make it multiplicative on their scorecards, not additive.

We all know it's a Best Practice to put diversity objectives on senior leaders' scorecards. While some companies balk at this because of potential misperceptions regarding quota setting, many other companies have adopted this practice and generated great results.

Instead of adding this to executive scorecards, consider the practice of using this as a multiplier. Their scorecards will still add up to 100%, without diversity metrics. They will have a diversity multiplier that could get them to 150% of their total score if they achieve their diversity goals. One hundred and fifty percent is 30 times five percent, thereby, chances are you will get the same multiplier in their engagement and attention.

ELIMINATE UNCONSCIOUS BIAS

Want to eliminate 100% unconscious bias in screening, and improve recruiter efficiency and effectiveness by 95%? Eliminate job requirements in postings and do not request resumes. We are familiar with the Best Practice of eliminating unconscious bias in job requirements and anonymizing resumes to avoid irrelevant information. Many companies are employing both strategies.

The problem with this approach is that applicants have figured out how to manipulate the system by using relevant keywords in their resume that increase the odds of being picked up by automated application management systems, and recruiters are still overwhelmed with too many candidate profiles that do not adhere to the job requirements.

Even better is the practice of not mentioning job requirements at all in the posting and putting a link to a 10-15 question survey with multiple choice answers that address the skills, knowledge, attributes, experience and education required for preferred for the job.

The survey takes 5-10 minutes to complete for the applicant, so it is not excessively onerous for them. The answers can be scored and tabulated to precent the candidates with the highest scores for next step in the recruiting process, without mentioning names, genders, colleges, geographies and other confounding information that create unconscious bias. The questions can even be weighted to reflect differences in relevance for job success.

Areas for further probing in the interview can be identified based on the answers to the survey. References can be asked the same questions later in the process, and their ratings can be checked against the applicant's self- assessed scores. And, for the selected candidates, subsequent job performance can be correlated to survey scores for predictive data that is useful for future job postings.

Dr. Suri Surinder is the CEO of CTR Factor Inc., Chief Learning Strategist for Diversity Learning Solutions and author of several leadership and diversity management e-books.

Embracing Our Growing Diversity

We are a country divided by identity: divided by rural and urban, by race and ethnicity, by sexual orientation, by abilities both physical and emotional, by gender, by economic opportunity, by immigrant status, by culture, by political viewpoint, by religion. Our identities are multiple and overlapping; many of these differences – these expressions of who we are – exist in the same person. These differences have made America strong. They have also caused Americans to be at odds with one another.

The demographics of the country have been rapidly changing for a generation. They will inevitably lead to a country which looks very different than it does today. But realize, our differences have always been here. There have always been people of color in America. People with disabilities and different sexual orientation. People who spoke different languages and had different cultural identities. People who were immigrants. People who were successful and people who were not. And people who thought differently about any number of things, social and political.

The difference now versus in times past is we talk about these things more openly and we are acknowledging them. We are realizing we need to deal with them to find solutions to the problems they bring us and create opportunities for the wealth they represent.

Accept it or not, any demographer will tell you America will continue this shift ,and people who look, act, think and celebrate differently are here to stay.

My message for my conservative friends, or my friends who are afraid of this change, or my friends who are uncertain about what this means for them is this: instead of resisting, instead of fear, embrace this difference. Learn what you can about who the people are that are different from you. They are, in fact, your neighbors and, often, fellow citizens who have the same rights, dreams, privileges and responsibilities as you.

And for my progressive friends who think they get this, who think their cultural competence is high, I have a message for you too, in fact, a challenge. How do we bring in the white person who feels left behind, for whom this is a zero-sum game, that if some win others must lose? These are real people who are also part of the diversity, equity and inclusion equation, deserving of our attention and concern. They cannot be seen as the enemy. This is the conundrum presented by the political and ideological divide in our country. We must solve this.

As a point of reference, I am a late middle-aged, white guy. But my grandchildren are a mix of white, Latin and African American. They are the future of America, just like the white children of the country. They are ALL our future. Because ultimately, whether you resist or embrace the demographic changes in our country, it is their future. Will your workplace and community welcome them? I sincerely hope so; so that we can all thrive in a diverse and changing world.

Steve Humerickhouse is the Executive Director for The Forum on Workplace Inclusion at Augsburg University.

Inclusion

The evolving paradigm of inclusion: Where are we headed?

Ableism. Latinx. Nonbinary. Alternative spirituality. Transracial. Mansplain. The landscape of diversity & inclusion is no longer Black and White, or Female and Male; it requires the ability to navigate culture in a manner that is vastly different today than ever before. But just wait until tomorrow!

Countless studies have shown that diverse employee representation at all levels of an organization has a quantifiable impact on financial performance. In fact, it is now commonly acknowledged that diversity & inclusion serve as the engine for many corporations to ensure the knowledge, critical thinking and innovation required to successfully achieve business and mission-critical objectives. But haven't we been talking about "the business case" for diversity & inclusion for some time? How much progress have we – diversity practitioners – really made in our corporations and more broadly throughout society? And does the next generation of diversity practitioners have a different agenda from that which we are immersed in today?

Diversity & inclusion started receiving widespread use throughout corporate America in the early 1990s. At the time, efforts to advance this work were largely compliance-related and focused on equal employment opportunity laws, which initially concentrated on limited protected classes. Fast-forward nearly 30 years later and we have made great strides. Or have we?

• Only two of the 300 case studies read by first-year Harvard Business School students include illustrations of Black executives. • In 28 states, there are no explicit statewide laws protecting people from discrimination on the basis of sexual orientation or gender identity in employment, housing and public accommodations. • Despite growth in recent years, only 6.6% of Fortune 500 CEOs are women. • Thirty percent of workers fits the federal definition of having a disability, yet less than half disclose that information to their employer which exemplifies the absence of a culture of inclusion and safety in the workplace. Last year, I tuned in to watch the reboot of comedy pioneer, Norman Lear's *All in the Family* and its spinoff series *The Jeffersons.* The live event recreated the original episode from both of the Emmy-winning comedies which debuted nearly 50 years ago. The brash comedy illustrated in both sitcoms played on the politically charged, and often times bigoted and sexist, environment of the time. Strikingly, amidst the contemporary backdrop of today's #MeToo, #LoveWon and #BlackLivesMatter movements, Archie Bunker is still relevant. The more things change, the more they stay the same.

Over the past 30 years, we have looked at diversity as an approach to foster representation and ensure access into the workplace. Moving forward, diversity emphasis will continue to shift toward strategies that drive equity, inclusion and social justice. When you focus on inclusion, diversity often comes naturally. Representation will also look different for tomorrow's workforce. We are already learning expectations from the newest generation to enter the workforce. Generation Zers self-identify as competitive, spontaneous, adventuresome and curious, not to mention multicultural with membership and belonging to various diverse communities. Investments from younger generations, and the positions they occupy, will affect how companies make business decisions. Transformation is an urgent business requirement, and cultural competency is fundamental to that transformation. Developing integrated business strategies to level the playing field across cultures with metrics such as employee engagement, customer satisfaction, impact on bottom-line, as well as retention and termination rates, will be instrumental to accelerating the development of culturally proficient and nimble organizations. Organizations that actively accelerate transformation are dedicated to fostering a work environment where people from diverse backgrounds work comfortably in teams. These organizations recognize that talent and ability are not limited, but enhanced, by the diversity and cultural expertise that individuals bring to the workplace. While we have made tremendous progress, we realize that diversity and inclusion is a journey, not a destination, where no one, myself included, knows everything there is to know about every single culture. Instead, we have to collectively develop the cultural humility to learn that which we do not know with the end goal of enhancing the level of respect, civility and dignity that we demonstrate to one another.

James E. Taylor, PhD, Chief Diversity, Inclusion, and Talent Management Officer, UPMC

From the Classroom to the Boardroom, Nothing Less than Your Best Will Do

On my first day at Head Start, I was nervous. Nervous about being in a new environment. Worrying if I'd make any friends. And, most of all, if I belonged here. Noticing my state, Mrs. Williams, our teacher, looked at me and said, "Miriam, you're a big girl now, you're where you're supposed to be."A rush of relief waved over me. And I never forgot that moment. Another moment from Head Start, a government-sponsored early -education program, that has stayed with me are the words my mother told me,: "Do your best."

"Do your best" simply means putting forth your best effort. In the classroom, it meant to respect others and apply my best effort to obtain the best grades possible. As I've progressed through life, so has my perspective of *doing my best.*

It now includes designing and implementing strategies and, most importantly, doing my best as a servant leader, wife, mother, daughter, sister, aunt, friend and neighbor. That phrase has installed a deep sense of personal accountability and self-awareness. When I reflect, as I often do, I ask myself, did you do your best? This healthy and vulnerable look in the mirror has had a lifelong impact on the way I contribute to my family, society and work. It's about putting forth a true and honest effort and consistency in everything that's important to me.

In today's competitive business environment employers are heavily investing in programs aimed at helping employees do their best work. Along with areas including culture and training, this work also falls under Diversity, Equity & Inclusion (DE&I).

DE&I, put simply, is a fancy (and perhaps 'trendy') way to say, "respect others".

All people - especially employees - want to be valued and respected. Equity is a form of respect and it must be integrated into key human capital progress, such as hiring, performance ratings, promotions, compensation and terminations. These are great starting points and are sustained by adding bias detectors to processes. The bias detectors help ensure equity or parity across all segments of the population. This is a key qualifier: to keep the focus on mitigating biases from processes; not merely raising awareness or telling people what the issue is without any solutions.

Equity and transparency in human capital processes yield greater organizational trust and employee loyalty, as well as increased financial results. DE&I is the secret sauce to business success - it is no longer optional. Successful DE&I strategies remove distractions and barriers, enabling employees to focus on the mission and deliver the desired results. In other words, to help them do their best.

In turn, when businesses do *their* best for all employees, they achieve growth and success in ways they did not think were possible. A prime example is the military. There is great transparency and equity in their people processes. Basic training, essentially a robust onboarding program, guards the culture and mission. And the oath taken to do their best to serve the country is never compromised - no matter who you are or where you come from, you are to protect the country, no exceptions.

What result could you deliver if all your employees were laser-focused on the mission and everyone was treated with the same level of respect and opportunity and trained to vet out invisible distractors such as unconscious bias? Would you outpace the competition? How much market share could you gain by allowing everyone to do their best?

DO your best is a simple statement, however,r when coupled with Diversity, Equity & Inclusion, it can yield tremendous results anywhere; even in the classroom and boardroom. The question is, are you ready to do your best to make this happen?

Miriam H. Lewis, Chief Diversity, Equity & Inclusion Officer, Principal Financial Group

Managing Bias

Removing Barriers to Women's Workplace Success

Hiring, retaining and advancing women into supervisory and management roles has been discussed for over 50 years, beginning with the passage of the Civil Rights Act of 1964. Thanks to the sexual harassment legislation enacted at the end of the 1970s, employers began to be held accountable for workplace practices that included hostile work environments, retaliatory behavior toward women who reported unwanted contact, and double standards for males who violated sexual harassment policies. In spite of these visible proactive strategies, in 2017 and 2018, we witnessed more women than ever come forward to call out sexual harassment through the #metoo movement, whistleblowing, and lawsuits alleging sexual discrimination.

Gender Microaggressions and Sexual Harassment—What's the difference?

On a daily basis, there are subtle workplace behaviors that affect women's sense of comfort, productivity and even safety. These have come to be known as microaggressions. Microaggressions are so commonplace or seemingly benign that they often go unnoticed, both by the perpetrators and the victims. They may even be masked as jokes. Yet these are behaviors that continue to frustrate women's goals of workplace advancement. Consider the following:

At work, this guy is always eyeing me up and down; it makes me feel awful.

During our team meetings, one guy invariably interrupts and talks over all of the women, even the team leader; why doesn't someone call him out?

I shared with my female colleague that her jokes about women were creating an unhealthy dynamic in the department; she told me I was being too sensitive and should join the #metoo movement.

Gender microaggressions are defined as brief and everyday verbal, behavioral and environmental behaviors that communicate demeaning, hostile and otherwise sexist insults towards women (Nadal, 2010). Nadal also describes three types of gender microaggressions:

Gender microassaults: blatant sexism — verbal, nonverbal and behavioral. For example, being verbally demeaning by calling a woman a "bitch" or a "whore."

Gender microinsults: Often unintentional behaviors and statements that still convey negative messages about women. For example, in professional meetings or classrooms, the convener may call primarily on men, although plenty of women are raising their hands to speak.

Gender microinvalidation: This takes many forms, such as exclusion from an activity because of a women's sex, negating a woman's ideas with jest, and ignoring the only woman in a room full of men, even though she is a coworker.

Swim, Hyers, Cohen, and Ferguson (2001) also call these behaviors "everyday sexism" because they occur so often that they then begin to be viewed as typical in that setting. We may all be in settings where everyday sexism is ongoing, yet we fail to notice. Instead, we make attributions such as: *That's just John, being John; don't take him seriously;* or *Carl is basically a good guy, just from an older generation; calling you sweetheart is not a big deal.*

Sexual Harassment or Gender Microaggressions?

About 20 years ago, a colleague and I developed a sexual harassment training program for a global firm on the East Coast. The leadership was very surprised to learn that their diversity survey results pointed primarily to issues of sexism rather than racism. Of course, both identity issues were intertwined, but nevertheless, the findings from women's comments were alarming. At the end of the survey, everyone was invited to comment (a standard practice with surveys), and comments from women raised red flags to the Directors of Diversity and Human Resources. Women wrote that they were "ogled" in the cafeteria, touched too much and asked to serve coffee, even if men in a meeting could do it for themselves. They also reported being humiliated by supervisors if they introduced an idea without sufficient data or asked for time off to pick up a sick child from school. The diversity survey also pointed to significant statistical differences in the way men responded to questions about workplace climate; in general, men's responses suggested that everyone was treated fairly and given the same opportunities.

Though survey findings are very useful because they provide baseline data against which later surveys can reference, nuances are often missed. Indeed, a cross section of women reported in later focus groups with this company revealed that they felt like they were in a hostile work environment — a form of sexual harassment — but that they decided to continue working without pursuing their concerns with HR. The survey, however, provided validation and gave them a voice, and the complaints to HR about what today are called gender microaggressions began to increase.

Considerations for employers

It is important to note that gender microaggressions or gender discrimination are not isolated to one identity phenomenon. Often, perpetrators also attack a woman's age, ethnicity and/or sexual orientation. Unfortunately, no work setting is immune to gender microaggressions. Quite often individuals engaging in microaggressions plead that it was "just a joke" or that they did not mean any harm. Yet microaggressions, if unchecked, can create a hostile work environment and a violation of workplace policies and Title VII of the Civil Rights Act of 1964.

In their article regarding perceptions of gender microaggressions in the workplace, Basford, Offerman and Behrend (2014) found that:

Witnesses of microaggressions, regardless of gender, perceive greater microaggression against women as the explicitness of the discrimination increases;

Witnesses also expect female targets to experience poorer work outcomes following more blatant microaggressions;

Women were significantly more likely than men to perceive gender microaggressions.

These findings suggest the importance of education, training and coaching as interventions that can benefit all employees and supervisors. The training programs I designed for different employers always began with participation by the organizational leaders. My premise is that in most organizations, change comes from the top. When managers and employees learn that the senior management team has participated in a training, they tend to be more trusting and less cynical when they are asked to attend an identical workshop on microaggressions and sexual harassment.

A good training program will include examining examples of gender microaggressions, a discussion of the effects of microaggressions and information for those employees experiencing microaggressive behavior in the workplace. Training should also emphasize the responsibility of supervisors to hold accountable those employees who perpetuate gender microaggressions. Reprimanding may not be easy for men to do with other men when it comes to gender microaggressions, but role-playing as part of the training can prepare male supervisors for this important task. Creating an inclusive workplace climate also includes gender-neutral but affirming practices, such as a manager opening a team meeting by inviting everyone to share an accomplishment from the week before, or having employees compliment someone in the meeting for a positive behavior they observed.

Employers seeking to manage and change their workplace culture must lead by example. To have a respectful and productive work environment, leaders must make diminishing gender microaggressions a priority. An educational workshop can go a long way toward achieving this goal by involving management and employees in new learning and advocacy for themselves and others.

Patricia Arredondo, Ed.D, President Arredondo Advisory Group

DIVERSITY RECRUITING POPULAR RESOURCES

Source: 2021 DMBA Inclusive Leadership Index

DIVERSE PROFESSIONALS	CAMPUS
National Black MBA Association, Inc	Undergraduate Internship Program
Prohispanica	Virtual Job Shadows
National Association of Asian MBAs	Student Organization Partnerships
ASCEND	Recruiters engage in HBCU development
National Association Black Accountants	Student Mentoring Program
ALPHA	ERG Matching Program w/ School Chapters
National Society of Black Engineers	Integrated Programs engaging students year-round
Society of Hispanic Engineers	Series on learning Industry
National Association of Women MBAs	Club-sponsored Events
Society of Women Engineers	Student Diversity Summits
VETERANS	**PEOPLE WITH DISABILITIES**
Recruit Military Veterans	Goodwill Industries
Military Airforce Bases	Nevins Center
Department of Veteran Affairs	University Child Development Institutes
Veterans Job Bank	Work Without Limits
GI Jobs	Disabled American Veterans
Vocational Rehabilitation	Disability Jobs.net
US Chamber Hire our Hero's	National Technical Institute for the Deaf
HIRE Purpose	State Department Rehabilitation Services
Military Officer Job Opportunities	Disability; In
University Veterans & Reserve Officers	Ability Jobs
LGBTQ+	**BIPOC (New)**
Reaching Out MBA	Program to Retrain Formerly Incarcerated
GLMA Gay & Lesbian	Governor's Council on Talent Pipeline for African Americans/ Blacks
ROMBA	Technical Apprenticeships
LGBTQ Chamber of Commerce	Community Partnerships to Train Talent
Time Out Youth	High School Partnerships to Access Talent
Out 4 You	Career Fairs in Under-Served Communities
LGBTQ Community Centers	Dedicated Role to develop BIPOC Talent Outreach
Hospital Networks	Partnerships with Social Services Agencies to Identify Talent
PRIDE Parades	University Partnerships Targeted at BIPOC
PRIDE Employee Resource Groups	Tools developed for leaders and managers to enhance communication & collaboration

BIBLIOGRAPHY

Breaugh, J. (2009). Recruiting and Attracting Talent A Guide to Understanding and Managing the Recruitment Process. SHRM Foundation

Choate, Andrea. Neuroleadership Lessons: Recognizing and Mitigating Bias in the Workplace, SHRM, HR People+Strategy, November 30, 2016.

Keating, Dan and Karklis, Laris, Nov.25 2016, Diverse Population Map

Kaplan & Nordan, 1992; Introduction of the Balance Scorecard, Harvard Business Review

Meshanko, Paul, 2013; Author The Respect Effect: Using the Science of Neuroleadership to inspire a more loyal and productive workplace

McElvane, Pamela A., Founder of Index (data reporting period: 12/31/2016- 2020) Diversity MBA Inclusive Leadership Index Benchmarking Report. www.diversitymbamagazine.com/methodology/benchmarking/

Miriam Webster, Illustrator; p.108

Nielsen Diverse Intelligence Series 2015 – www.nielsen.diverseintelligenceseries.com; www.nielsendiverseintelligenceserieslgbt

United States Census – 2016, 2010 – uscensus.gov

Veterans Jobs Mission: veteransjobsmission.com

The SkiNy on Diversity Recruiting is a timely, real-world guide for those who seek to recruit diverse talent. As a data-driven roadmap for navigating the intersection of talent management and diversity, equity, and inclusion, this book offers solutions that are grounded in actionable insights. Pam McElvane is a passionate thought leader in the DEI space, and her book lays out a step-by-step path for recruiting in a multicultural world.

—**Kirsten Marriner,** EVP, Chief People & Corporate Affairs Officer, The Clorox Company

The SkiNy on Diversity Recruiting is a comprehensive and customizable resource that will benefit every organization's diversity recruiting efforts, regardless of their inclusion milestone. It provides tangible insights and tactical steps for today's competitive talent environment. Every reader will come away having had an enriching experience.

—**Marsha Jones, EVP,** Chief Diversity & Inclusion Officer, PNC Financial Services Group

As the ongoing war for talent intensifies, organizations will be required to develop and execute holistic acquisition strategies to attract and employ a workforce that meets the challenges of an ever-changing marketplace. The increasing diversity, broadening skill sets and expectations of the today's workforce demand a sharpened focus in this area if organizations are to establish and maintain competitive advantage."

—**Eugene Kelly,** Vice President, Global Diversity, Equity & Inclusion, Colgate-Palmolive Company

Diversifying the talent pipeline is a laser-focus for Board members and C-Suite executives. Pam McElvane has created a compelling blueprint that brilliantly outlines strategies for recruiting top, diverse talent. This is an outstanding resource that will elevate your organizational capabilities related to sourcing, talent acquisition, and measurement. Elevated capabilities lead to significant IMPACT!"

—**Fernando G. Little,** Chief Diversity Officer – Atrium Health

This book is a must-read! As corporate America's premier "DEI Whisperer", Pam McElvane shares insights and best practices on diversity recruiting that will take your DEI efforts to the next level." This book is the resource guide every hiring manager and recruiter must have in their toolkit. Even, better anyone looking to create a recruiting plan this is a road map and resource for you.

—**Keith R. Wyche,** Walmart Stores & Best-Selling Author, *Diversity is Not Enough*

The SkiNy on Diversity Recruiting is chock-full of relevant data, actionable insights, and best practices to help any organization achieve success in its diversity initiatives. This is a step-by-step guidebook for all leaders seeking to achieve a competitive advantage from a diverse employee base."

—**Sharmila Fowler-Pos,** Head of Diversity - Echo Global Logistics

Made in the USA
Monee, IL
23 September 2023

43198960R00077